HANDBOOK OF MARINE SURVEYING

HANDBOOK OF MARINE SURVEYING

THOMAS ASK

WATERLINE

First published in the UK in 1998
by Waterline Books, an imprint of Airlife Publishing Ltd

British Library Cataloguing-in-Publication Data
  A catalogue record for this book
  is available from the British Library

ISBN 1 84037 034 3

The information in this book is true and complete to
the best of our knowledge. All recommendations are
made without any guarantee on the part of the publisher,
who also disclaims any liability incurred in connection
with the use of this data or specific details.

Typeset by Phoenix Typesetting, Ilkley, West Yorkshire
Printed in Great Britain by WBC Book Manufacturers, Bridgend, Glamorgan

Waterline Books
an imprint of Airlife Publishing Ltd
101 Longden Road, Shrewsbury, SY3 9EB, England

In loving memory for my parents *Anne Marie* and *Johan*.
In loving affection for my wife *Beth Ann*.

Contents

Introduction

Our desire to walk off the land and slip onto the water has thrust boats into a cherished category of mechanical things. Boats have allowed us to harvest the seas, explore new lands, escape from oppression and find serenity. Boats put us into an unnatural environment and therefore draw from us an intense trust. This utter dependence we place in our boats requires us to appreciate their design and integrity. A marine survey will ensure a boat is in good condition and will confirm the vessel's inventory is sufficient to handle emergencies.

The intent of this book is to develop a solid foundation of knowledge upon which experience and skill can be developed. It is much more important to understand likely causes for troubles and common areas from which they originate than to list frequent problems experienced on a given boat design. For example, among all the words on theory and technique, the reader will find that most problems relate to fatigue, corrosion (along with its wooden cousin, rot) and overloading at stress concentrations. Every boat will experience these and one of the informal rules of thumb during a survey is to assume these problems exist and keep looking until you find them. You will rarely be disappointed.

Upon identification of problems, one must ponder whether the problem is serious and consider the best course of repair. There are two principal responsibilities a surveyor has to the client. They are 1) evaluation of the structural integrity of the vessel, and 2) evaluation of the safety equipment. This is a short list but must always be kept in mind so that the cracks in the corner of the fibreglass settee do not rise to the level of separated bulkheads or a loose keel. Structural integrity is perhaps a vague description but it includes all the items that keep a boat safely afloat such as the hull, deck, keel, ribs, stringers, bulkheads, engine bed, chain plates, mast steps, standing rigging and all the fasteners that keep them connected.

Safety items are usually dictated by statute, but a short list of critical items includes bilge pumps, fuel system and fire extinguishers. The ability to thoroughly investigate structural

integrity and safety items is the minimum requirement for a merely adequate surveyor. Beyond these minima lie the many parts, pieces and systems that make a boat operate efficiently. Pointing out broken hinges and kinks in the potable water line may not seem important but they should be a natural outcome of a good survey.

Surveying is not glamorous. Headfirst contortions into malodorous bilges and the inadvertent burying of hands into piles of decaying rodents have been part of the business for me. However, a love of boats, a desire to ensure the safety of their passengers and crews along with personal integrity are sufficient ingredients to motivate the surveyor into the unpleasant, never-visited corners of a boat. Some areas will truly be listed as 'inaccessible for inspection' but this is a defeat for the surveyor and should rarely be used. Unfortunately, even the most careful surveyor cannot always identify and prevent problems related to fatigue, crevice corrosion, metallurgical problems and inaccessible areas. The burden of addressing these types of problems lies fully with the boat designer. The designer must provide preventative maintenance scheduling for all critical components. These can be based on operating environments (e.g. salt water vs fresh water, pleasure vs workboats, etc.) but it is impossible for a surveyor or boat owner to consistently and reliably know when such things as the keel bolts, standing rigging, hull-to-deck fasteners and bedding need to be replaced. The replacement schedules for these items are based on engineering analysis and experimentation, both of which are not the responsibility of the surveyor.

Just as providing poor preventative maintenance specifications is an evasion of responsibility for the boat designer, it is an equal wrong for the surveyor not to make conclusions about the vessel's condition. For example, the survey can register a long list of cracked features in the deck, but is the deck seaworthy or not? Are repairs to these cracks required, recommended or cosmetic? That is, the surveyor must make conclusions on behalf of the client. Deep cracks in the coamings and some gel coat cracks in the hull do not mean the boat is a dangerous wreck. In the same manner, a gleaming, sailing yacht with a poorly supported, misaligned keel is a disaster waiting to happen.

Careful consideration must be given to predicting the loads that are carried by every part of the boat. For example, how strong should a filter bracket mounted on the engine pan rail be? After evaluating the 'g' forces generated by engine vibrations and the weight of the full filters, the answer is: the filter must be strong enough for a heavy mechanic to stand on when he services the turbocharger on top of the engine. How strong should a fire extinguisher bracket adjacent to the companion way be? Strong enough to support one end of a wet clothes-line. The designer and the surveyor should expect all of these 'unexpected' applications.

Primers

Material Mechanics

An object moves when a force is applied to it. It either accelerates to some sort of equilibrium speed or, if it is restrained, the object itself moves by compressing (or stretching). The way an object moves internally is the key to understanding a material's behaviour. Every type of material has a unique way of stretching or compressing. The relationship between the force and the movement of the material defines how it can be used.

A ten-pound (4.5 kg) weight hung on a rubber cord would stretch the cord very far. If the same ten-pound (4.5 kg) weight were hung on a one inch diameter steel rod, there would be no noticeable stretch (even though it actually stretches 0.0000004 inches per inch (0.00001 mm per mm) length of the steel – more on this later). Neither of these materials would break but it is obvious which one should be used to support an overhead hoist.

Although a force can only produce tension, compression or shear it is convenient to think of loads being applied to an object in five ways: tension, compression, shear, torsion and flexure. Tension is simply a force that

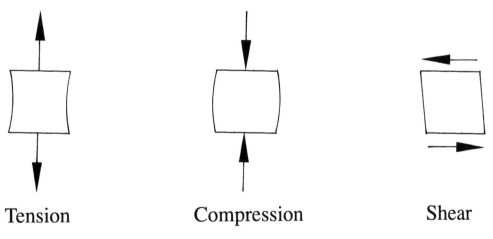

Tension	Compression	Shear
Pulls molecules apart.	Squeezes molecules together.	Slides molecules over each other.

Figure 1   Loading conditions

pulls apart an object. Compression is the opposite of tension and is the squeezing of an object. Most materials have a higher compressive strength then tensile strength. Shear is a set of opposing forces in the same plane. For example, if the bottom of a plate is rigidly attached to a surface and then the top of the plate is pushed parallel to the surface, a shear force will be applied to the plate. The shear force comes when the force at the bottom of the plate resists the force on top of the plate. These opposing forces are transmitted as a shear force in the plate. If the plate were made from a stack of papers, the shear force would readily allow the papers to slide across one another.

Torsion is a twisting force. For example, a rod that is held rigid at one end while a rotating force is applied at the other end will experience a torsional force. Flexural loading is a convenient way to describe the unique loads produced on a flexed object. If a bar is supported at both ends and a load is applied in the centre, the material on the same side of the centreline as the load will be in compression whereas the material on the opposite side of the load will be in tension. In addition, the stress varies with the distance from the centreline. The outer skin has the highest stress and the centreline will have zero stress. This loading condition is explained in further detail in the 'Primer on Composite Materials'.

In addition to the reaction of a material to a load, another important characteristic of a material is its behaviour as it is about to break. Some materials are brittle and hardly stretch before they break. Glass is the most common example of a brittle material. Other materials, like wood, are ductile and stretch noticeably before they break. This characteristic determines the existence of common warning signs (bending or stretching) prior to imminent failure.

A force's effect on a material is dependent on the size of the area upon which the force is applied. The force per area is called *stress* and is simply equal to force divided by area.

$$\sigma = F \div A$$

Where,
 σ = Stress
 F = Force
 A = Area

Strain is the same as stretch or compression but refers specifically to the movement per unit length. Stress-strain diagrams have been developed for most materials by taking a sample of the material and applying force on it while monitoring its length. The force is continually increased until the sample breaks. Figure 2 shows an example of a stress-strain diagram.

Most materials in boat construction are *linearly elastic*, that is, over a certain range of stresses the strain is directly proportional to the stress (*Hooke's Law*). Moreover, when the stress is removed, the materials return to their original unstressed dimensions.

The slope of the stress-strain line is called the *modulus of elasticity* (or *Young's modulus*) and is equal to the difference in stress divided by the difference in strain. This number indicates the rigidity of a material.

$$E = \sigma \div \varepsilon$$

Where,
 E = modulus of elasticity
 σ = Stress
 ε = Strain

What happens to a material as the stress is continually increased? The *elastic limit* or *yield strength* is reached, beyond which the material continues to stretch but will not completely recover if the stress is removed. This permanent stretching (called *yielding* or *plastic strain*) at stresses above the elastic limit occurs in what is called the *plastic region*. As the stress is further increased, the material finally breaks. This point is called the *ultimate strength*.

Where does the material for the stretching come from? In the elastic region, the stretching comes from the increased distances between atoms. In the plastic region, groups of atoms (crystals or grains) slip or deform to allow the stretch. As the material strains in one axis, it also strains in the perpendicular axes. This intuitive relationship is denoted by the ratio of strains called the *Poisson's ratio*.

Table 1

Moduli of Elasticity

Tensile at 70°F (21°C)

Material	× 1,000,000 psi	GPa
Steel	30	206
Stainless steel	30	206
Brass/bronze	16	110
Aluminium	10	69
Grey cast iron	20	138
Monel	26	180
Titanium	16.5	114
Magnesium	6.5	45
Osmium	80	552
Nylon	0.4	2.8
Polyethylene	0.014 to 0.18	0.096 to 1.24
Rubber	0.0006 to 0.50	0.004 to 3.4
Plate glass	10	69
Wood	1.5	4.6
Concrete	3	9.2

Consider some of these practical implications of the relationship between stress and strain:

• Nearly all product designs are based on the yield strength. That is, all considerations of safety factors, fatigue strength and impact loading are based on a value that will allow the material to completely recover from the applied stress. Notable exceptions are armour and crash cushions where the energy of the impact is absorbed by taking the material up to or beyond its ultimate strength.

• The modulus of elasticity determines the flexibility of a material and is independent of its strength. However, an object's shape is the most important determinant of its flexibility. For example a thin stick blows readily in the wind whereas a thick limb made of the same wood does not move at all. (See 'Primer on Composite Materials' for more information on the effect of shape on rigidity.)

• The area under the stress-strain curve indicates a material's toughness or energy absorption ability. The larger the area, the more energy the material can absorb before it breaks.

• Unlike metals, typical composites do not have the same stress-strain characteristics in all axes (known as *anisotropism*) therefore, the modulus of elasticity and yield strength will be different depending on orientation. If a load is pulling in the same direction as the fibre orientation it will be much stiffer and stronger than if it is pulling perpendicular to their orientation. With a perpendicular load the fibre strength is basically unused and only the resin offers resistance to the load. Metals and other *isotropic* materials have the same stress-strain relationships in tension, compression and shear.

A material's hardness is another characteristic that has practical importance in determining a part's strength and wear characteristics. Hardness is defined as the resistance to penetration and is directly related to the material strength. Metal hardness is usually changed by various heat-treating processes that modify the grain structure.

Thermal expansion is linearly related to the temperature and is caused by an increase in the vibratory movement of atoms. The amount of expansion varies by material and is

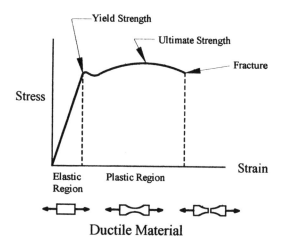

Ductile Material

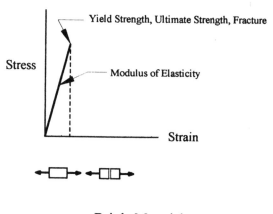

Brittle Material

Figure 2   Stress-strain diagrams

measured by the *thermal expansion coefficient*. Brass has a thermal expansion that is 50 per cent more than that of steel and

Table 2

Coefficients of Thermal Expansion

at 70°F (21°C)

Material	Expansion Coefficient in/in/ °F	mm/mm/ °C
Steel	0.000006	0.000011
Stainless steel	0.000009	0.000017
Brass/bronze	0.000009	0.000017
Aluminium	0.000012	0.000022
Cast iron	0.000005	0.000009
Monel	0.000008	0.000014
Magnesium	0.000014	0.000025
Graphite	0.000003	0.000005
Polyethylene*, high density	0.000066	0.000119
Polyvinyl chloride*	0.000031	0.000056
Polycarbonate*	0.000040	0.000072
Nylon*	0.000056	0.000101
Plate glass	0.000005	0.000009

* Varies widely based on specific composition.

aluminium is twice that of steel as shown in Table 2.

If two materials expand into each other, either because they have different thermal expansion coefficients or are at widely different temperatures, they develop stresses directly related to the strain they produce. That is, the strain produces stress rather than the other way around.

Failure Modes & Analysis

A part has 'failed' when it does not perform its function. This is true even when the part is not broken. For example, a hinge has failed if it heats up and expands during operation, causing a linkage to lock up. Specifically, the hinge was subject to a temperature induced elastic deformation failure. This semantic review is necessary in order to introduce the precise terminology of failure analysis. The following paragraphs describe common failure modes. In many applications, failure is often the result of several concurrent effects. These combined effects can lead to failures at stresses well below the maximum strength of a material, as is the case with *fatigue* and *stress corrosion cracking*.

In identifying the cause of failure on a boat, the methodology of *root cause failure analysis* should be followed. This basically involves the following steps:

1. Identify the *primary failure*, that is, the first component that failed. This failure may have led to secondary failures that are irrelevant to finding the root cause of failure.

2. Learn about the circumstances around the failure. What happened to make the part fail? How were loads applied? How old is the part?

3. If the primary failure was the breakage of a component, inspect the surface where the break occurred, referred to as the *fracture face*. This face will give an indication of the ductility of the material as well as whether the failure was due to an overload or fatigue.

4. Although not done as part of a survey, metallurgical or chemical analysis can reveal whether the material is defective. Detached, irregular cracks in metal parts are usually caused by a material defect. This type of cracking should not be confused with intergranular corrosion (see 'Primer on Corrosion').

5. Consider all the information gathered and determine the root cause. For example, if a part has been in service longer than recommended by the manufacturer and subsequently failed due to fatigue, poor maintenance would be considered the root cause of the fatigue failure.

Failure Modes

Elastic Deformation

This failure mode is caused by a load on a part that is high enough to distort the part and make it stop functioning. The load can be caused by an external force or thermal expansion. The load in the case of elastic deformation failure distorts the material within its elastic range. That is, the stress that is induced by the load is low enough that the material recovers completely when the load is removed. If the stress is higher than the yield strength of the material, it will stretch and never recover. If the stress exceeds the ultimate strength of the material, the material will break. It is worthwhile to note that ductile materials, such as steel, stretch a great deal before a ductile rupture occurs. Brittle materials, such as glass and fibreglass fibre, do not yield before a brittle fracture occurs. Consequently, ductile materials give warning signs before they break while brittle ones do not (see 'Primer on Material Mechanics' and 'Brittle Fractures' below).

Yielding

Yielding occurs when the applied force exceeds a material's yield strength. A part which has yielded is stretched, distorted and is close to breaking.

Ductile Rupture

Under a continually increasing load, a ductile material will elastically deform, yield and then finally rupture. A ductile rupture is caused by the slow growth of internal cracks under a load. The cracks grow together until the part breaks. The fracture face will usually be rough and have a "torn out" appearance. This is due to the load shearing up and down between the grains.

Brittle Fracture

Unlike a ductile material, a brittle material has little yield and can therefore dangerously fail without warning. A brittle fracture is caused by the rapid separation of interatomic bonds. The internal voids and cracks that are always present in materials initiate this fracture. In brittle materials, the stress concentrations produced by these features cannot be distributed (see 'Primer on Stress Concentration'). The fracture face of a brittle fracture will usually appear as a flat, crystalline surface and may show chevron-shaped beachmarks that point to the failure origin.

A brittle fracture can occur in normally ductile materials at low temperatures (below the *transition* or *glass temperature*) or when they have been subjected to *stress corrosion cracking* (see 'Primer on Corrosion'). The motive to understand steel's behaviour at low temperatures is rooted in marine experience. Several steel-hulled ships plying cold waters

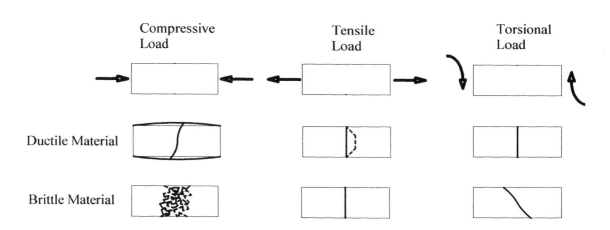

Fracture characteristics of ductile and brittle rods under compressive, tensile and torsional loading

Figure 3   Fracture characteristics of shaft

were literally cracked in half before the cause and solution were understood.

When the temperature of a metal is below this transition temperature, a crack can travel faster than the metal can deform. Because deformation normally absorbs tremendous amounts of energy, a low-energy crack that does not produce deformation can propagate readily. This phenomenon occurs principally with steels because of its unique *face-centred cubic* crystalline structure. Copper, aluminium and nickel have a *body-centred cubic* crystalline structure and their mechanical properties are not very sensitive to temperature. Generally, the smaller the grain size the lower the transition temperature. Plastics also experience this phenomenon (see 'Primer on Plastics').

Figure 3 shows the typical fractures of ductile and brittle shafts under different load conditions.

Fatigue

Fatigue is by far the most common cause of mechanical failure. Described in detail in the 'Primer on Fatigue' section, fatigue is a failure mode caused by cyclic action of a part resulting in failure at a below-normal stress. A fatigue fracture will show two distinctive surface appearances. One of these areas will exhibit curved ridges or *beachmarks* that were produced as cracking slowly progressed through the object. The other surface will usually be rougher and show no distinct pattern. This rougher surface is created when the object was so weakened by the fatigue that it ruptured quickly.

Impact

Impact is a very rapidly applied load. Stress waves, produced during rapid loading, actually stack up on each other thereby amplifying the stress.

Buckling

Buckling occurs in parts that have a very low thickness to length ratio. Buckling is a common failure mode in thinwalled tubing and unsupported reinforcement fibres. It will occur at stresses much lower than the compressive strength of the material.

Thermal Shock

This failure is well described by its name. It is caused by such large differences in thermal expansion within a material that it fractures or yields.

Wear

Wear is the result of one object contacting another, leading to the removal of material. Wear is not necessarily due to the ploughing of the object, specifically referred to as *abrasive wear*, but can also be due to adhesion of two mating materials. This adhesion causes surface cracks that grow and eventually cause small flakes of material to break away. This type of wear is called *galling* and if the wear continues, the galling will lead to seizure of the two wearing parts.

Cavitation is an erosive wear caused by the formation and implosion of bubbles. In the case of propellers, a low pressure area being formed behind a propeller blade causes cavitation. The low pressure area allows the water to boil. When the water vapour recondenses it implodes and wears material away.

Brinelling

Brinelling fractures occur when two curved surfaces are excessively loaded so that yielding occurs over the small contact area. The most common example of brinelling is observed in ball bearings that have had an excessive radial load applied to them. This loading forces the balls against the race with sufficient force to brinell the surface and leave small dents in it.

Spalling

Spalling is caused by cracks developing between the grains or crystals of a material. The cracks grow until particles flake off.

Spalling often results from brinelling or high temperatures.

Corrosion

Corrosion is the biggest instigator of part failures in marine applications. Corrosion is the electrochemical attack of a material and is described in the 'Primer on Corrosion'.

Consider the following scenario involving the separation of a forward bulkhead from the deck. Suppose an investigation finds no evidence of impact loading; such as might occur in a docking collision or dropping from a cradle. The separation was initiated at the point of highest loading, high flexibility and/or unusually high stress concentration (of course the 90-degree bend at the connection is a source on its own). Moreover, the connection was sound for a long time and there was no evidence of poor resin bonding. Given these facts, the root cause would probably be fatigue failure due to the design life of the joint being exceeded by the number of hull twisting cycles.

Corrosion is typically found at the base of masts

Stress Concentration

A sudden change in an object's dimensions, such as a sharp corner, notch, hole or crack will result in an increase in stress in this area. The mathematical analyses of these stress concentrations are so complex that their amplifying values are obtained experimentally. The following graphs relate part shapes to the corresponding stress concentrations. The relationship between shape and stress concentration illustrates the importance of gradually blending mating surfaces.

Perhaps it is internal stress concentrations developed in the voids and cracks of normally-produced materials that have allowed the advent of materials fabricated from tiny particles to be so much stronger than the normal, parent form. Metals and ceramics crushed into particles of less than four millionths of an inch (two hundred thousandth of a millimetre) in diameter are being used to fabricate very strong objects. When the 'nanopowders' are compacted they can be as much as ten times stronger than their parent material.

A graph of stress concentration versus radius sharpness is shown in Figure 4.

When assessing a boat, develop an understanding of how loads are distributed. With this feel for load distribution, give special attention to sources of stress concentrations that could be exposed to heavy or cyclic loads. Understanding where stress concentrations are produced is important in understanding where failures are most likely to originate.

When a crack is formed, the ends of the crack produce a stress concentration. It is accepted practice to drill small holes at each end of a crack to reduce the stress concentration in this area and to stop the crack's progress. This drilling is done before repairs are made. In some applications, small metal

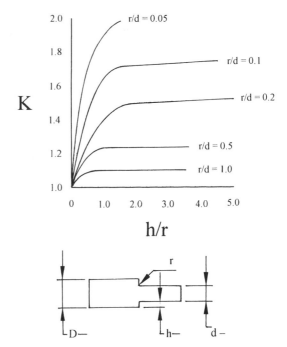

Stress Concentration Factors (K) for bending of flat bar with geometry portrayed above

Figure 4   Stress concentration factors

cracks in non-critical areas are treated in this manner and no additional repairs are made.

Ductile materials are less sensitive than brittle materials to stress concentrations. As a ductile material is loaded, it can deform to redistribute the load over a broader area. Even though the brittle form of a material can handle higher stresses, a ductile material can distribute stress and therefore actually bear a higher load.

Fatigue

As a material is heavily loaded and unloaded, its maximum strength decreases. This gradual weakening is called *fatigue*; a name derived from an early misunderstanding of this phenomenon. The metal was thought to have become 'tired' over time. It is now understood that fatigue is caused by tiny movements between grains that cause cracks to propagate through the grain boundaries. One solution to fatigue is to over-design an object. Generally, if the stresses experienced by an object under cyclic loading are less than half the yield stress, the object will never fail due to fatigue. However, over-designed objects waste natural resources, labour and money. Therefore, highly efficient designs are produced only when the anticipated loading and fatigue characteristics are fully understood.

When watching the constant twisting of hull and rigging, one can only wonder, 'how long can it take that?' The onus for determining the fatigue life lies with the designer. Acoustic emissions and other advanced techniques are not available to the surveyor in evaluating the initiation of fatigue. However, there are some visual clues that may help diagnose imminent failure. Fatigue failures often start at sources of stress concentration or at the surface of an object where the stresses are usually highest. Small surface cracks may be the first sign of fatigue. Then again, there may be no visible cracks. They may be too small to see, start from inside the object, or be obscured. For example, the stress concentra-tion at the corner of a shaft keyway is a common location for fatigue cracking. This area cannot be observed unless the shafted assembly is completely torn apart.

Inspecting a broken object subject to fatigue failure will always show two different surface characteristics: 1) the *fatigue zone* where cracks slowly propagated into the object and 2) the *instantaneous zone*, where the crack accelerated quickly through the object. The relationship between the size of the fatigue zone and the instantaneous zone indicates the relative loading of an object. The instantaneous zone is produced when the effective area (total area minus fatigue zone) is too small to support a load. Therefore, if the instantaneous zone is small, the object was not heavily loaded. However, if the instantaneous zone is large, the object was heavily loaded.

The fatigue zone is identified by beachmarks which are small ridges on the broken surface of a material. These beachmarks are produced by the crack propagation and plot the crack progression. Due to abrasion within the crack, older fatigue zone areas are smoother than new ones and can help identify the failure origin.

Fatigue Strength

Although *fatigue strength* is not directly related to any other material property, it is most closely related to tensile strength. Corrosion, galling and other surface defects reduce a material's resistance to fatigue more

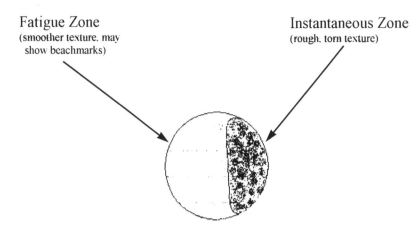

Fatigue Zone
(smoother texture, may
show beachmarks)

Instantaneous Zone
(rough, torn texture)

Figure 5 Fracture face of
fatigue failure

than can be attributed to stress concentrations alone. Consequently, fatigue strength is usually determined experimentally. It is also interesting to note that metals that are repeatedly yielded become *work hardened*. This makes the metal harder and more brittle. When a paper clip or wire is bent back and forth until it finally breaks, it has been made more brittle by the process and finally snaps.

Fretting fatigue

Fretting fatigue is a special form of fatigue that is initiated by the small vibrations of parts that are pressed together. The vibrations cause surfaces to crack. These cracks produce stress concentrations that accelerate the fatigue of the parts. Fretting fatigue often occurs at pressed joints which are not intended to move. It can be readily reduced in these cases by decreasing the clearance between the fastener and the through hole or by using higher strength and correspondingly higher tightening torques. In the same vein, it should be noted that impact loading that may result from oversize holes due to design or wear is undesirable because of the stress amplification produced.

Creep and Thermal Relaxation

Creep is a term used to describe the gradual stretching of a material under a load.

Although it is most common in unreinforced plastics, it happens to some degree in metals also. Creep is due to slippage of a material's crystals or grains along their boundaries. This generally is not a concern except with highly loaded plastics that require dimensional stability and materials subject to high temperature. *Thermal relaxation* describes creep that is accelerated by high temperature.

It is important to remember that both fatigue and creep occur at stresses *lower* than the yield strength of a material. This means, for example, that a propeller shaft or shroud can crack and break under normal loads after many years of reliable service. It is equally important to note that corrosion of any sort greatly decreases fatigue strength. In fact, a part that has had pitting corrosion machined off will have much higher fatigue strength, even with the large loss of material, than the original part with the pitting.

The solution to fatigue failures is preventive maintenance. Fatigue life can only be determined by experimentation and a preventive maintenance schedule of critical components must be offered by the boat manufacturer to properly ensure their reliability.

24

Corrosion

Corrosion is the nemesis of mariners. Because of their rapid corrosion, the hard steels available on land were slow in reaching marine applications. Massive bronze, brass and iron structures were used in their stead. It seems that everything touching seawater quickly weakens due to the deleterious effects of corrosion. The advent of plastics, stainless steels and nickel alloys has provided great immunity from the continual corrosion process. Corrosion ranks with fatigue as the most common cause of material failure. However, they usually work together – what corrosion starts is often finished by fatigue.

In 1780, the Italian anatomist Luigi Galvani hung some recently-killed frogs from copper hooks. To his surprise, the frogs' legs started to kick! As it happens, the copper hooks were connected to an iron rod. Fortunately, Galvani knew that an electrical current would produce the same reflex action in the frog legs and therefore he connected the reflex action of frog legs with the unintentional and macabre phenomenon he observed on the copper hooks. This 'animal' current, as it was originally called, led to experimental investigations into the remarkable phenomenon of *galvanic corrosion* and our current understanding of corrosion.

Anodes and Cathodes

All corrosion results from two materials exchanging electrons. Metals have loosely attached electrons and will readily give them up to other materials. The material that gives up electrons, and consequently loses material, is called the *anode*. The material that receives the electrons is called the *cathode*. The electrons move through an *electrolyte* such as water. The propensity of a material to give or receive electrons from another material is determined by the electrochemical nature of the material.

A sacrificial anode of zinc protecting a large cathode, such as a steel hull, dramatically illustrates the effect of donating electrons. The hard, strong zinc is quickly eaten up by this continuous transfer of electrons. This flow of electrons is in fact an electrical current and this galvanic corrosion is used to great advantage in batteries.

Galvanic Cells

Steel, oxygen and water produce the most common galvanic cell. Rust is caused by the iron in steel reacting with the oxygen in water or air. These molecules combine to form the nonwater soluble rust. The reaction sequence is described below:

$$Fe \rightarrow Fe^{3+} + 3\,e^{-}$$

(An iron atom dissolves, creating an iron ion and three free electrons. This reaction actually occurs in two steps.)

$$4\,e^{-} + 2\,H_2O + O_2 \rightarrow 4(OH)^{-}$$

(Four free electrons coming from the iron reactions, two water molecules and one oxygen molecule react to form four hydroxyl ions.)

$$Fe^{3+} + 3(OH)^- \rightarrow Fe(OH)_3$$

(The iron ion reacts with three hydroxyl ions to form one insoluble rust molecule.)

Oxygen forces nearby metals (which readily shed electrons) to become anodic. Because of their higher electrode potential (a relative measure of their naturally occurring voltage with respect to hydrogen, see Table 3), zinc and magnesium can protect steel because they dissolve into water more readily than does iron and therefore donate electrons more readily than does iron.

In other words, the following zinc and magnesium reactions occur more readily than the dissolving of iron that was previously discussed:

$$Zn \rightarrow Zn^{2+} + 2\,e^-$$

(A zinc atom dissolves, creating a zinc ion and two free electrons.)

$$Mg \rightarrow Mg^{2+} + 2\,e^-$$

(A magnesium atom dissolves, creating a magnesium ion and two free electrons.)

The electrons contributed by the zinc or magnesium then react with the hydroxyl ions produced by the solution of oxygen.

The naturally-occurring electrical potential difference is shown by the listing of electrode potentials with respect to hydrogen as shown in Table 3. The driving force for these reactions is the voltage difference between them. This series is basically the same as the galvanic series.

Galvanic Corrosion

Galvanic corrosion is typically used to describe corrosion due to dissimilar metals.

As discussed previously, this type of corrosion, like rusting, is caused by one material donating electrons to another. The materials behaving as anodes weaken as they give up electrons to cathodic materials. Consequently, mating materials need to be matched by their electrochemical nature or galvanic relationship. Some metals such as stainless steel, aluminium and titanium can be *passivated* by isolating the metal from the cathode. In stainless steels the chromium is strongly attracted to oxygen and forms a protective oxide layer. In a similar manner, aluminium and titanium both react with oxygen to form a thin protective oxide layer. These passivations reduce the rate of corrosion but do not eliminate it. The coatings are susceptible to chemicals that will strip the oxygen away and destroy the oxide coatings. Unfortunately chloride, which is a part of seawater, is one of them. This is why aluminium and stainless steel should be routinely washed with fresh water.

Stray current corrosion or electrolysis is caused by two or more objects charged with a different electrical voltage. This is a reverse form of galvanic corrosion but works much faster. This is a helpful process when used to plate materials. The part to be plated is connected to the cathodic side of a DC voltage source and the part that will donate its molecules is attached to the anode. Poor grounding of electrical equipment and crossed grounds are the most common causes of stray current corrosion. Crossed grounds means that the negative terminal of a battery is used as the ground on some equipment and the positive terminal on others. Stray current corrosion can also be caused by currents flowing in the water, such as might occur in a marina.

Table 4 lists common materials and their relative galvanic relationships in seawater. The further apart the metals are on the table, the greater the galvanic action and subsequent corrosion. This is why graphite is used

26

with zinc in dry cell batteries. The table shows some metals in their position when passivated. The loss of the passivation will make them much more anodic.

Table 3

Electrode Potential

(volts at 77 °F (25 °C), 1 molar solution)

Reaction Potential   *Electrode*

MOST ANODIC

Reaction	Potential
$Mg \rightarrow Mg^{2+} + 2\,e^{-}$	-2.36
$Al \rightarrow Al^{3+} + 3\,e^{-}$	-1.66
$Zn \rightarrow Zn^{2+} + 2\,e^{-}$	-0.76
$Cr \rightarrow Cr^{2+} + 2\,e^{-}$	-0.74
$Fe \rightarrow Fe^{2+} + 2\,e^{-}$	-0.44
$Ni \rightarrow Ni^{2+} + 2\,e^{-}$	-0.25
$Sn \rightarrow Sn^{2+} + 2\,e^{-}$	-0.14
$H_2 \rightarrow 2\,H^{+} + 2\,e^{-}$	0 (reference)
$Cu \rightarrow Cu^{2+} + 2\,e^{-}$	+0.34
$4(OH)^{-} \rightarrow 4\,e^{-} + 2\,H_2O + O_2$	+0.40
$Fe^{2+} \rightarrow Fe^{2+} + e^{-}$	+0.77

MOST CATHODIC

Al = Aluminium	Ni = Nickel
Cr = Chromium	O = Oxygen
Cu = Copper	Sn = Tin
Fe = Iron	Ti = Titanium
H = Hydrogen	Zn = Zinc
Mg = Magnesium	

Table 4

Galvanic Series of Common Alloy Groups

MOST ANODIC

Magnesium alloys
Zinc
Aluminium alloys
Cadmium
Carbon steel
Cast iron
Lead-tin solder
Lead
Tin
Brasses
Copper
Bronzes
Tin
Nickel-copper alloys
Stainless steels
Titanium
Hasteloy C
Platinum
Graphite

MOST CATHODIC

This galvanic table gives generalised positions of alloys in seawater. Many subtleties exist such as the position of passivated stainless steels. Although their electrochemical natures are nearly the same, their order, starting with the most anodic is:

Chromium steel (e.g. Type 401)
Chromium-nickel steel (e.g. Type 304)
Chromium-nickel-molybdenum steel (e.g. Type 316)

Table 4 illustrates some of the following points:

• Brass and steel hardware should not be mixed.

• Bronze propellers and bushings need to be protected from stainless steel shafts.

- Aluminium will slowly corrode around steel fasteners and very rapidly corrode around brass fasteners.

- Zinc and magnesium can be used to protect steel, brass, bronze and almost any other material.

- Graphite is more cathodic than any other material it contacts.

Galvanic action is accelerated with increased electrolyte conductivity. Therefore, galvanic corrosion increases with increases in temperature, salinity and pollution. Electrolyte conductivity is much higher in seawater than in fresh water. It is worth highlighting the fact that the edges of threads expose a lot of surface area and will most quickly show galvanic corrosion.

Stress Cells

Microscopic galvanic corrosion can actually occur within an alloy where two different grain compositions are present such as in aluminium alloys. Corrosion can also be initiated by *stress cells* in which the stressed part of a material acts as the anode and the unstressed part acts as the cathode. This can be seen in metals that have been formed by such processes as bending or stamping.

Crevice Corrosion and Pitting

Small crevices and cracks between a material can restrict the free movement of an electrolyte and lead to an electrolyte that has a different composition in the far reaches of the crack. This system is called a *concentration cell*. Many different types of concentration cells exist depending on the composition of the materials. However, the *oxidation-type concentration cell* is one of the most common and is a typical cause of *crevice corrosion*.

As discussed previously, one of the naturally-occurring chemical reactions is the process of oxygen reacting with water and consuming electrons. This reaction actually occurs in both directions, that is, oxygen, water and free electrons react to produce hydroxyl ions while hydroxyl ions will react to produce oxygen, water and free electrons in order to achieve equilibrium. This back and forth reaction is shown with a bidirectional arrow:

$$2\,H_2O + O_2 + 4\,e^- \leftrightarrow 4(OH)^-$$

The electrochemical force that creates the hydroxyl ions is weak so not many are formed. The quantity on each side of this equation is governed by the *Le Chatelier's Principle* which states that the balance will move in the direction that reduces stress. For example, if a lot of oxygen is added to the solution, more hydroxyl ions will be produced to counteract the change.

This reaction shows that when oxygen reacts to form hydroxyl ions, it draws electrons from nearby metals. These nearby metals where the oxygen concentration is lower (and hydroxyl concentration is higher) must provide electrons for this reaction and therefore become anodic. And like a sacrificial anode, the stripping of electrons causes them to corrode. Consequently, in the case where the flow of the electrolyte is restricted, causing oxygen concentrations to vary, the apparently contradictory situation arises of the metal exposed to lower concentrations of oxygen corroding faster than the metal exposed to higher concentrations.

Concentration cells are important phenomena because they produce corrosion in difficult to view areas such as underneath

Example of pitting in a stainless steel nut

Example of the rapid wasting of aluminium when located near brass

Example of corrosion of steel under a brass nut

fasteners, clamped joints, scale, dirt, cracks, barnacles and algae. Moreover, this accelerated corrosion in stagnant crevices can eat deeply into a small area of the material and make it weaker than the surface condition or weight loss indicates. Crevice corrosion is a bigger concern with metals that rely on passivated coatings for protection such as stainless steel and aluminium.

Like crevice corrosion, *pitting* can deceptively weaken a material. It is initiated without a crevice and occurs randomly over the surface of a metal. Pitting becomes more prominent than overall surface corrosion in metals that either have a high alloy content or develop protective oxide coatings.

Intergranular Corrosion

Many alloys are also subject to *intergranular corrosion* which shows as a web of cracks. The composition of the grain may be different from the grain boundaries, resulting in a lack

Crevice Corrosion

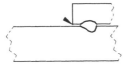

Stress Corrosion Cracking

Pitting

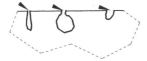

Various Types of Corrosion
(shown in cross-section)

Both pitting and crevice corrosion are similar to the galvanic corrosion of dissimilar metals. Stress corrosion cracking is produced by the combined effects of tensile stress and corrosion

Figure 6   Crevice and pitting corrosion

of protection for the latter material. For example, some stainless steels will have too low a concentration of chromium at the grain boundary due to a low amount of this alloy, or its preferential affiliation with carbon, to prevent the grain boundaries from corroding like carbon steel.

Stress Corrosion Cracking
Stress corrosion cracking is caused by a combination of tensile stress and intergranular corrosion. The material stress may be produced either externally or by residual stress produced during manufacturing (e.g. punching). Stress corrosion cracking creates the dangerously surprising condition in which a normally ductile material fails in a brittle manner.

Biological Corrosion
Biological corrosion is a special form of corrosion resulting from interactions between a material and living organisms. Bacteria, fungi and mould can excrete acids that chemically attack a material.

Corrosion Characteristics
The following summary describes the most common forms of corrosion in various metals commonly used in marine applications.

Stainless steel
Stainless steel is susceptible to pitting and crevice corrosion. Stainless steels with a low chromium, low nickel or high carbon content are the most susceptible to corrosion.

AISI 316 / BS 316S31 is the best choice in stainless steels for typical marine applications because it contains 3 pecent molybdenum that provides additional corrosion resistance.

Aluminium
The biggest corrosion problem with aluminium is pitting. Probably the most pitting-resistant aluminium alloy is ANSI 6061 or BS H20 while ANSI 2024 or BS/DTD 5090 is the least resistant. ANSI 5052 or BS 2L55 a is commonly used aluminium alloy in marine application. Because aluminium is anodic, when it corrodes it basically dissolves away, although a white, crusty scale usually develops.

Bronze and Brass
When submerged in salt water, bronze and brass will readily corrode when in contact with steel or aluminium often leaving a rough, green appearance. Bronze and brass are also susceptible to the weakening effect of *dezincification,* which is the leaching of zinc from a material. Dezincification can produce a bright copper colour. It can be resisted by the addition of inhibitors such as arsenic, antimony and phosphorus. Brass will also react with ammonia, a common component in cleansers, producing a blue-green corrosion. Phosphor bronze, aluminium bronzes as well as red and admiralty brass work well in a marine environment.

Nickel alloys
Nickel alloys are virtually impervious to corrosion. However, pitting is possible with some alloys.

Cast Iron
Cast iron will rapidly form a rust surface that bonds to the underlying iron. The bonded rust does not readily flake off (as occurs with steel) and provides corrosion protection for the iron. The bonded rust is brown-coloured but can look almost black when submerged in water. Nickel and silicon cast irons have the best corrosion resistance, however all irons have very good resistance.

Steel
Unpainted or uncoated carbon steel will rapidly rust, especially when subjected to salt. The rust is coarse textured and flaky.

Polished and hardened steels corrode more slowly than do unfinished steels and many paints and coatings now permit steel to be used successfully in marine applications. A special form of carbon steel called *weathering steel* does not flake like normal carbon steel. Instead, the oxide produced during rusting produces a fine textured, adherent barrier to oxygen in the same manner as cast irons.

Evaluating Design Features

Because corrosion is such a big problem on boats, the following summarises favourable design features that reduce corrosion:

- Material selection should balance corrosion resistance and economy. Fortunately, plastics have allowed hulls and other components to be liberated from corrosion at a low cost.

- Avoid galvanic couples.

- When materials cannot be galvanically matched, fasteners should be more cathodic than their surrounding metal. Fasteners are much smaller than the material they connect, therefore if one of these items is going to galvanically corrode, it should be the fastened material because it can sustain the material loss better than the fastener. Thus, brass and stainless steel are good fastener material whereas aluminium – especially the ubiquitous aluminium pop rivet must be carefully employed.

- The anodic metal in a dissimilar metal connection should not be coated. A small break in the coating would allow the exposed anodic material to rapidly corrode under the influence of a much larger cathodic area.

- Sacrificial anodes should be used liberally.

- Component design should reduce the number of crevices that can hold precipitated salt or allow for crevice corrosion. Silicone sealants are cheap and highly effective in preventing moisture from entering crevices such as rigging terminals.

Wood

'I've known some ships made of dead trees outlast the lives of men made of the most vital stuff of vital fathers' declared Captain Ahab in Herman Melville's *Moby Dick*. Wood has always been a trusted and predictable material. A well-placed screw or additional lashing of rope will quickly cure any faults. The clipper ship's wooden hull and spars carried the tens of thousands of square feet (thousands of square metres) of sail that drove them more than 20 knots.

Wood has the distinction of being the oldest and only renewable construction material in boats. Its predictable characteristics are due to its ductility and easy to see grains. Even wood's creaking and groaning offers a natural status monitor and warning sign. (Normally the unique sound characteristics, or *acoustic emission*, that a material generates when loaded must be electronically processed in order to determine its condition.) However, wood has many problems in marine applications. It has a poor strength to weight ratio and is susceptible to rot and worm infestation.

Wood is a cellular material. Specialised cells provide structural support, transmit sap or store food in the living tree. Wood cells are composed of *cellulose, lignin, extractives* and *ash-forming minerals*. Seventy per cent of wood is composed of cellulose. Lignin acts as the adhesive matrix for wood. The ash-forming minerals constitute less than one per cent of the wood and contain the stored nutrients for the tree. The extractives are not part of the wood structure but produce the characteristics of colour, odour and decay resistance. They include tannins, starch, oils, resins, fats and waxes.

A cross-section of a tree shows two differently coloured regions. The lighter, outside ring is *sapwood* and the darker inside core is *heartwood*. Sapwood is usually less than two inches (5 cm) thick. However, with ash, hickory, maple, and some pines the sapwood ring may be up to six inches (15 cm) thick. The sapwood consists of living cells that transport sap. The heartwood is older sapwood in which the cells have become inactive. The heartwood often contains minerals that give it a darker colour. In addition, the heartwood of ash, hickory and some oaks have much of their porosity plugged by naturally occurring ingrowths. The mineral content and plugged pores can give heartwood uniquely different characteristics than sapwood. White oak heartwood is used for liquid storage barrels because of its natural sealing. Another attractive characteristic of heartwoods is their better resistance to organic attack.

Wood is anisotropic and the strength in the direction of the grain is approximately ten times higher than in the direction parallel to the grain. That is, the grains can be pulled apart much easier than they can be broken along their length. This characteristic is accounted for by good design practice or by

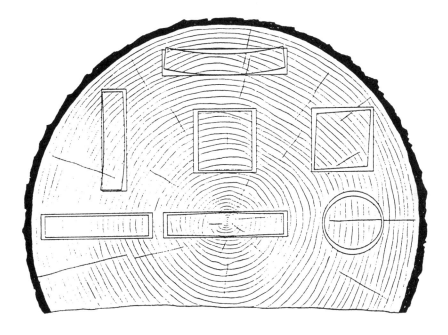

Figure 7   Wood warpage

layering sheared plies at right angles as is done with plywood. Wood also warps readily in a direction radial to its original growth. Quarter-sawn lumber is the best cut because the grains run straight through the plank and will not warp.

Determining the load-carrying ability of wood is based on numerous factors. Wood strength is decreased with the increasing presence of knots and other discontinuities (e.g. shakes, checks, and splits) as well as rot and moisture content. Again, the grain direction is the most important influence on strength. Laminated wood reduces the effect of knots by spacing them out across the wood and reducing the likelihood that they will penetrate the entire laminate. Wood also has the unique characteristic of becoming weaker the longer a load is applied.

Wood is frequently glued to add tremen-dous strength to a screwed fastening. Glues or resins bond tenaciously to wood and distribute the joint loading over the entire joint rather than the area around the fasteners. Epoxy resins are excellent for adhering all kinds of wood, whereas polyester resin should not be used on redwood and close-grained woods like oak or cedar.

Plywood

Plywood is an important material in boat construction. Although its use is declining, it is still used in many marine applications and is an excellent, low cost, easily worked material. Plywood is a composite material consisting of thin layers of wood that are shaved off rotating logs in a very efficient lathe process. Plywood is usually made from Douglas fir although it can be made from almost any wood, including hardwoods.

Knots in the plies are filled and the plies are then glued to a low-density wooden core. The plies are oriented so that the grain direction is the same on either side of the core. The next layers of plies applied have their grains at right angles to the underlying ply. This process of applying plies of alternating grain directions on either side of the core is repeated until the desired thickness is achieved. The outermost plies are called the faces or veneers and give the plywood its finished appearance. Knot-free faces with an attractive grain are the most expensive type of plywood.

The advantage of alternating the ply grain direction, as discussed in the 'Primer on Composite Materials', is to give the plywood equal strength along two axes. Equally important for plywood, is that the opposing grain directions improve the dimensional stability of the composite. Plywood will not distort or warp nearly as easily as wood will when it absorbs moisture.

Balsa

Because balsa wood is a commonly used coring material and is not encountered by the surveyor in any other function it is worth some special discussion. Although balsa wood is very soft it is actually classified as a hardwood. It only weights 11 lb/cubic foot (176 kg/cubic metre) compared to 35 lb/cubic foot (561 kg/cubic metre) for Douglas fir, and 57 lb/cu ft (913 kg/cubic metre) for oak. Balsa can be harvested in only six years and is principally composed of large sap-filled cellulose cells. Unfortunately, it will decay if left lying on the ground for a couple of days and is therefore, promptly dried to minimise the chance of fungal decay. Balsa wood is bonded with glue because it does not hold fasteners well. Balsa needs to be cut and worked with sharp knives and shears rather than conventional woodworking equipment.

Damaging Organisms

Rot

Although wood weathers at a very slow rate, fungi-producing rot and marine borers can quickly damage it. In all its forms, wood rot is identified by discolouration, lifting of paint and by penetration testing with an awl. Rotted areas will be easily penetrated with an awl point. Rot is somewhat contagious and as an organic substance, spreads its microscopic veins further down the wood grain than what appears to be the affected area. The fungal attack that causes rotting starts out by creating a very slight staining or wet appearance. As the decay increases, the colour change is more obvious – white if the fungi consume lignin and cellulose and dark if the fungi feed primarily on cellulose.

Fungal growth occurs when the wood is suitably moist and the temperature is between 50–90°F (10–32°C). The growth is fastest when the wood moisture content is slightly above its saturation point. Dry wood and water-saturated wood will not rot. Air-dried wood typically contains less than 20 per cent moisture and is safe from fungus. It is the immersion and drying cycles of boats that creates an attractive environment for fungal growth.

As previously mentioned, the heartwood of some species is more resistant to rot than the sapwood. Sapwood however will absorb preservatives more readily. The heartwoods of the following trees are considered to have a naturally high degree of rot resistance.

Bald Cypress
Black Locust
Black Walnut
Catalpa
Chestnut
Cedars
Iroko
Junipers
Makore

Mesquite
Osage orange
Pacific Yew
Red Mulberry
Redwood
Teak

Oak is a common boat construction material and is reasonably resistant to rot but it is not in the same league as the above mentioned woods

Marine Borers

When the Greek navy launched their ships to meet an invading Persian fleet in 480 BC, the Greek vessels proved to be more nimble and manoeuvrable than the Persian ships. This allowed more rapid turning and faster acceleration, which in the age of ramming triremes was their key ammunition. The Greek ships won the battle and protected Greece and its renowned culture from the onslaught of these marine invaders.

The manoeuvrability of the Greek ships was in part due to the fact that they were afloat for a shorter period of time than the well-travelled Persian ships. The Greeks had launched soon before the battle whereas the Persians had sailed all night and consequently were more waterlogged. In ancient days, ships were often beached to allow them to dry out. This was not due to the small amount of water absorbed by sound wood but rather the tremendous quantity allowed in by the actions of the ubiquitous shipworm.

The channels bored into wood by shipworms greatly increases the surface area of the wood available for absorption. Additionally, the channels themselves fill with water. Water is two to three times more dense than wood. All this added weight forces the vessels to ride lower which subsequently amplifies all the absorption problems. An unprotected 40-ton wooden vessel may have an additional one ton of normal surface water absorption and nine tons of water weight due to moderate worm infestation.

Shipworms are a species of worm-like molluscs. Shipworms are one species of marine borers that also includes the *limnoira*, *martesia* and *sphaeroma* species. When free-swimming shipworms find wood (which they only have 96 hours to do or they will die) they attach themselves to it and start boring. Twin boring shells located on their head grow as they nourish their way through the wood. The tail stays attached to the entrance hole by a lining of shell-like material. Although they can achieve a length of four feet (1.2 m), when numerous worms are present they will only grow a few inches (8 cm). The other species of marine borers are also molluscs but do not bore as deeply as shipworms. They are, however, pernicious organisms that frequently result in the destruction of untreated pilings.

The best way to identify worms is by the weeping of moisture that often accompanies their entrance holes on the wood's surface. When there is severe infestation, the surface wood will appear in good condition but the wood will be unusually easy to penetrate with an awl. Shaving away of the surface wood is the best way to find worm holes.

The heartwoods of the following trees have good resistance to marine borers.

Azobe
Greenheart
Jarrah
Kasikasi
Manbarklak
Teak
Totara

Teak is still a common deck and trim wood on yachts and has a good track record for both rot and worm resistance – teak structural timbers over one thousand years old have been found. Boats made entirely of teak are still produced in Southeast Asia where the huge leaves of the teak tree are still seen in the relatively plentiful, planted groves.

Other Organisms

Termites, carpenter ants and beetles also cause wood damage. However, these insects generally need to have permanent connection with the soil so they are not a common problem for boats.

Plastics

Plastics have overwhelmed the marketplace. They have evolved from a delicate, speciality material to tougher-than-steel wonders. Because of the generality of their name, they are limited in part by old-standing memories. At one time plastic denoted cheap and 'plastic' things always seemed to snap easily on cold days or even slight loading. Plastics had to a large degree earned their poor reputation in marine and other industrial applications. Unfortunately modern, high-performance plastics share the same name but are entirely undeserving of the cheap connotation. They have opened up so many design options that we are hard pressed to use them in all the applications begging for them.

Plastics are usually based on long repeating molecular arrangements called *mers*. This term is the root of *polymers* – the technical name for plastics. Plastics have the same structure as all organic substances. They are composed of long chains of carbon atoms with hydrogen atoms branching off the carbon atom. Additional atoms are attached to these mers to give them their unique characteristic. For example, polyvinyl chloride (PVC) has a chloride atom attached to its mer. The molecular structure of organic molecules can be seen in everyday life. Their hydrocarbon structures can easily be altered by heat. When wood, bread, PVC pipe or other organic structures are heated they become charred. That is, the hydrogen atoms linked to the outside of the hydrocarbon chain are driven free, leaving only the dark-coloured carbon backbone.

The *glass transition temperature* of plastics is usually higher than for metals and therefore must be carefully considered. The glass transition temperature (or simply *glass temperature*) is the temperature at which the molecules cannot rearrange themselves when a load is applied. Therefore, at temperatures below the glass temperature, the plastic becomes rigid and brittle.

Polymers have an inherent spring-like tendency due to the offset angles that bond the atoms. The amount of 'springiness' is usually controlled by the amount of interconnection between the mers. As the mers become more interlocked, they change from *elastomers* to *thermoplastics* and finally to *thermosets*.

Polymers can be developed into a three-dimensional structure during initial fabrication. The three-dimensional structure makes the movement of molecules difficult when heated; therefore, once formed they do not soften at high temperatures. Consequently, they cannot be moulded. This type of polymer is called a thermoset. Thermoplastics on the other hand have a linear, two-dimensional molecular structure and readily soften at high temperatures. Therefore these polymers can be easily moulded and will only hold their shape when cooled.

Natural rubber, silicone, nitrile, viton and other flexible materials are called elastomers.

The glass transition temperature is especially important in elastomers because their desired quality of flexibility will completely disappear. In fact a rubber band that has been frozen in liquid nitrogen can easily be snapped like a piece of glass.

Marine applications are an especially good use for plastics because of the need for corrosion resistance including concerns about galvanic relationships. Plastics are non-conducting and therefore will not corrode and can insulate dissimilar metals. Moreover, marine applications generally operate over a temperate temperature range. Using plastics in marine applications may reveal some of their common shortcomings such as the weakening effect of ultraviolet light, water absorption, dimensional instability, creep and poor impact resistance. However, many plastics will not exhibit any of these problems. The main problem with most plastics is their poor performance at high temperature and, more important for boat applications, their flammability and propensity to generate a lot of putrid smoke.

New versions of plastics are entering the market every day. The old standby 'commodity' plastics (polyethylene, polypropylene and polystyrene) and 'engineering' plastics such ABS (acrylonitrile butadiene styrene) and nylon have been tremendously enhanced over the years. Newer entries with complicated chemical designations and equally odd trade names have added even further to plastic's penetration into the marine industry. A few examples include the acetal Delrin® with its low water absorption, good wearing characteristics and machinability. The polyetherimide Ultem® is a high strength, high temperature plastic with good smoke and flame resistance. Centrex® and Hivalloy® weather well and maintain their colour and attractive lustre. Many other plastics are commonly used and most can be modified to provide such enhancements as ultraviolet light resistance and internal lubrication. Moreover, the strength of almost any plastic can be increased by adding small, randomly oriented fibre reinforcements.

Table 5

Mechanical Strength of Plastics

Material	Yield Strength, ($\times 1,000 psi$)	Tensile (MPa)
Polyethylene, high density	3	21
ABS	6	41
Polycarbonate	9	62
Polyester	10	69
Ultem® 7801*	25	172

* Example of 'high performance' composite plastics. This composite plastic can handle temperatures up to 414°F (212°C). It contains 25 per cent carbon reinforcement and therefore conducts electricity.

Metals

Strong, reliable and the namesake for great Ages of history, metals produced the first industrial revolutions. In marine applications, metals were quickly employed as fasteners, wearing components and anchors. Like wood, metals present appealing lustres ranging from the rich warmth of polished gold to the crusty slag of wrought iron that belies the maelstrom of fire from which it originated.

Steel and Iron

Heavy steel and iron structures evoke an oddly instinctive trust in their strength and durability. However, buried deep within their crystalline structures can lie tiny flaws that can dangerously weaken the metal. Before quality standards were entrenched, careful builders such as Washington Roebling, who built the Brooklyn Bridge, would require each lot of steel to be tested. Tragically, even these extraordinary measures were not enough. Fraudulent testing led to bad steel being used in the Brooklyn Bridge, causing a steel support cable to break and kill two workers. In fact the sinking of the *Titanic* may have been due in part to impurities in the steel, although she was sunk by the gashes produced by her well known impact with an iceberg south-east of Newfoundland, Canada. The leading theory for the steel plate's failure is that the steel had a high level of sulphur impurities. The sulphur, accompanied by the frigid water temperatures, made the steel very brittle and subsequently more likely to be damaged in the collision.

Melting iron ores such as hematite, magnetite and taconite produces steel and iron. These ores are either reduced to pig iron for steel production or made directly into cast iron. Steel refineries take the pig iron produced from blast furnaces and convert it to steel by burning out carbon and removing impurities in a steel refining furnace or converter operation.

Carbon is the key element in determining steel characteristics. A small increase in carbon content greatly increases strength and hardness but reduces ductility. With low ductility, cold forming processes like stamping become more difficult. As carbon content increases into the range of cast irons the only way to produce shapes is to melt and cast the iron. Cast irons are generally defined as 'steel' containing more than 2 per cent carbon. The bulk of steel consumption falls in the range of low carbon steel. These steels contain less than 0.3 per cent carbon and are interchangeably referred to as 'low carbon' or 'mild' steel.

Carbon content is so important in determining steel characteristics that it is embedded in its standard nomenclature. For example, a popular cold-rolled steel is referred to as 'AISI 1020' or 'BS 040A20'. AISI is the acronym for the American Iron and Steel Institute and BS stands for British Standards. The '20' in these designations indicates the steel has a carbon content of 0.20 per cent.

Many additives are routinely added to steel to ensure quality. For example, to remove crack-promoting sulphur, a small amount of manganese is added to combine with any residual sulphur. Silicon is also added to prevent oxygen from dissolving into the steel grains and making them brittle. Many other elements such as aluminium, cobalt, copper, lead, molybdenum and tungsten are added to steel to develop specific properties. These steels are often referred to as 'high alloy' steels. Chromium alone or chromium and nickel produce alloys known as 'stainless' steels. Steels without any of these special alloys are called 'carbon' steels.

Stainless Steel

Invented in 1930, stainless steels have provided the same reliable characteristics as steel without the problem of rapid corrosion. The term 'stainless steel' was actually a trade name for the new chromium-nickel steel alloy. The easy-to-remember trade name has stuck. The most common type of stainless steel that would be encountered in marine applications is the 300 Series. The 300 Series includes chromium and nickel in the steel that combine to give the alloy excellent corrosion resistance. This Series of stainless steels is very weakly attracted by magnets (referred to as *paramagnetic*) – notably different than the eagerly-magnetised carbon steels. The 300 Series cannot be heat-treated therefore it cannot be hardened like the other stainless steel Series. For example, low chromium versions of the 400 Series can be heat-treated and are commonly used in cutlery. The 400 Series is strongly attracted by magnets (referred to as *ferromagnetic*). This magnetic attraction challenges the time-honoured method of differentiating stainless and carbon steels. However, most stainless steel fasteners and components on boats are made from 300 Series stainless steel so the easily observed difference in magnetic attractions is usually an accurate method of differentiating between stainless and carbon steel. Stainless steels have a 30 per cent higher thermal expan-

sion coefficient and a third of the thermal conductivity of carbon steels.

Common commercial grades of stainless steel include:

AISI 304 or BS 304S31

Contains a maximum of 0.08 per cent carbon, 18–20 per cent chromium, 8–10 per cent nickel and 2 per cent manganese.

AISI 316 or BS 316S31

Has higher corrosion resistance than 304, especially to acids. It contains a maximum of 0.08 per cent carbon, 16–18 per cent chromium, 10–14 per cent nickel, 2 per cent manganese and 3 per cent molybdenum.

AISI 303 or BS 303S31

Contains 0.15 per cent carbon, 17–19 per cent chromium, 8-10 per cent nickel, 2 per cent manganese and 0.15 per cent sulphur. The sulphur is added to allow for easier machining. This grade is often used for fittings and other objects that require fine machining.

Alloy modifications of these common stainless steels are often made and are noted by the addition of a letter. The most interesting for our consideration are AISI 304L/BS 304S11 and AISI 316L/BS 316S11. These steels have very low carbon content with a maximum of 0.03 per cent. These are used for high temperature applications (see 'Primer on Corrosion').

Aluminium

Although extracting aluminium is a very energy intensive process, the raw material is all around us. In fact, 8 per cent of the earth's crust is aluminium. Typically it is extracted from bauxite, the richest aluminium ore commercially available. Aluminium is a popular fabrication material and is well known for its lightness. It is also renowned for its ability to develop a highly polished lustre. Like steel, there are numerous alloys of aluminium that are intended to produce a wide range of properties. Alloys are designated by a Series and Temper code.

Summary of Aluminium Series Groupings

1000 Series
Nearly pure aluminium, they are commonly used in electrical and chemical applications.

2000 Series
Copper is the principal alloying element. Copper improves the strength of the alloy. However, it does not have good corrosion resistance and is subject to intergranular corrosion. 2024 is commonly used for aircraft components.

3000 Series
Manganese is the principal alloying element. 3003 is a commonly used alloy because it combines strength, low cost and formability. Formability is the ease in which a material can be bent, stamped or otherwise deformed. It reflects a wide difference between the yield and ultimate strength.

4000 Series
Silicon is the principal alloying element. The silicon lowers the melting point so it is commonly used for welding wire. Some of these alloys can be treated so that they turn a dark grey colour. These alloys are popular for architectural applications.

5000 Series
Magnesium is the principal alloying element. Magnesium is more effective than manganese in improving the alloy strength. Moreover, these alloys have good resistance to corrosion and are probably the most common aluminium alloy in marine service.

6000 Series
Magnesium and silicon are the principal alloying elements. This series combines the attractive characteristics of strength, corrosion resistance and formability and can also be readily heat-treated.

7000 Series
Zinc is the principal alloying element. High strengths can be achieved with these alloys and they are used in the aviation industry for highly-loaded components.

The temper designations usually start with an H or T. H tempers indicate that the alloy was strain-hardened and T tempers indicate heat-treatment. The *Machinery's Handbook* and

Table 6

Aluminium Alloy Compositions
(percentage)

Alloy ANSI	BS	Silicon	Copper	Manganese	Magnesium	Chromium	Zinc
2024	DTD 5090	4.4	0.6	1.5			
3003			0.12	1.2			
4045	N21	10.0					
5083	N8			0.7	4.4	0.15	
6061	H20	0.6	0.28		1.0	0.20	
7075	L95		1.6		2.5	0.23	5.6

DTD is the acronym for Directorate of Technical Development.

other references provide detailed explanations of the temper designations.

Common aluminium alloys are shown in Table 6.

Brass

Brass is one of the most attractive and cherished alloys in the marine trades. It is corrosion resistant, easy to mould and machine and also has well appreciated aesthetic values. Brass is an alloy of copper and zinc that offers an unusually attractive combination. Not only does this combination of elements increase strength, which typically occurs with an alloy, but it also increases the alloy's ductility. Usually, ductility decreases when a high strength alloy is produced.

The major families of brass are the copper-tin-zinc alloys (this includes the red and yellow brasses), manganese bronze alloys (another yellow brass), leaded manganese bronze alloys and copper zinc silicon alloys (this includes silicon bronze).

Table 7 shows the composition of common brass alloys.

Table 7

Brass Compositions
(percentage, actual composition and trace elements vary)

Alloy	Copper	Zinc	Tin	Lead
Gilding brass	95	5		
Commercial bronze	90	10		
Red brass	85	15		
Admiralty brass	71	28	1	
Cartridge brass	70	30		
Yellow brass	65	35		
Free machining brass	61	36		3
Muntz metal	60	40		
Naval brass	60	39	1	

Bronze

Bronze was traditionally an alloy of copper and tin. However, the true definition of a bronze is an alloy of copper and any material besides zinc or nickel. The copper-tin alloys are very similar to brass in many respects. However, alloys of copper with aluminium, beryllium and silicon produce some special characteristics. For example, aluminium bronzes can be heat-treated to obtain relatively high strength. Copper beryllium is also heat-treatable, very strong, will not spark and has outstanding fatigue resistance. Silicon bronze such as Herculoy® and Everdur® are very strong. The major families of bronzes are the copper-tin alloys (tin bronzes), copper-tin-lead alloys (leaded tin bronzes), copper-tin-nickel alloys (nickel is not a major alloying element) and copper-aluminium alloys (aluminium bronzes). Manganese bronze includes zinc as a major alloying element and therefore is a brass. Copper-nickel alloys are actually a separate category of copper alloys that are very resistant to corrosion and are described further in the nickel section. Copper-nickel-zinc alloys (nickel silvers) fall into their own special category.

Typical compositions of bronze are shown in Table 8.

Nickel

Nickel-copper alloys with more nickel than copper are called monels. If the nickel content is only 12 to 30 per cent, it is called a cupro-nickel. The typical commercial monel is two-thirds nickel and one-third copper. All nickel-based alloys have outstanding corrosion resistance – the monels in particular.

Monels and most other nickel alloys can be differentiated from stainless steels by shaving the metal with a knife. Monels will shave like lead whereas the harder stainless steels will not shave at all. Monels are also much denser than stainless steels.

Nickel is often the contributor to alloys that creates amazing characteristics. Ranging from the Nilvar alloy (nickel and iron) with its tiny 0.000001 in/in/ °F (0.000002 mm/mm/°C)

Table 8

Bronze Compositions
(percentage, actual composition and trace elements vary)

Alloy	Copper	Tin	Zinc	Other Major Elements
Beryllium bronze	98			2 Beryllium
Silicon bronze*	92		1.5	4 Silicon
Tin bronze	88	10	2	
Leaded-Tin bronze	88	6	4.5	1.5 Lead
Aluminium bronze	88			9 Aluminium, 3 Iron
Manganese bronze*	64		26	4 Aluminium, 3 Iron, 3 Manganese

*Actually a brass

Table 9

Nickel Alloy Compositions
(percentage, actual composition and trace elements vary)

Alloy	Ni	Cr	Fe	Mo	Al	Ti	Other Major Elements
A Nickel	99.5		0.15				
Permanickel	98.6		0.10			0.5	
Duranickel	94.0		0.15		4.5	0.5	
Monel 400	66.0		1.35				31.5 Copper
Inconel 600	76.0	15.8	7.20				
Inconel 700	46.0	15.0	0.70	3.8	3.0	2.2	28.5 Cobalt
Inconel X-750	73.0	15.0	6.75		0.8	2.5	
Incoloy 800	32.0	20.5	46.0		0.3	0.3	
Hastelloy A	53.0		22.0	22.0			2.0 Manganese
Hastelloy C	59.0	16.0	5.0	16.0			4.0 Tungsten

Ni	=	Nickel
Cr	=	Chromium
Fe	=	Iron
Mo	=	Molybdenum
Al	=	Aluminium
Ti	=	Titanium

thermal expansion to the inconels (nickel-chromium-iron) that have been used for such high temperature, high strength applications as the fuselage of the X15 aircraft.

Common nickel alloys are shown in Table 9.

Magnesium

Magnesium is two-thirds the density of aluminium. This is its most significant advantage. It is used where weight is important but titanium is too expensive or difficult to process. Magnesium chips will ignite and have been used in incendiary bombs.

Titanium

Titanium has the best strength to weight ratio of any metal and is best known for its feats in the aerospace applications. Titanium is corrosion resistant – especially to seawater

and acids. Commercial alloys have a yield strength similar to the 300 Series stainless steels. However, exotic alloys can have a yield strength of 200,000 psi (1,378 MPa).

Zinc

Commonly used for galvanising (see 'Primer on Corrosion') it is also used to make exquisite, high definition die castings used as deck hardware and fittings. In this application it is usually chrome plated. Zinc melts at 787°F (419°C) and boils at 1,665°F (907°C) so it is easy to work with but cannot be welded at a high temperature as with arc welding. The loss of zinc in brass through boiling is an important consideration in processing brass. Processes such as casting or brazing may reduce the zinc concentration in an alloy.

Table 10

Mechanical Strength of Common Metal Alloys*

Material	Typical Alloy	Yield Strength Tensile × 1,000 psi (MPa)	Ultimate Strength, Tensile × 1,000 psi (MPa)
Magnesium	SAE AM265C	11 (76)	27 (186)
Aluminium	ANSI 3003-H14	21 (144)	22 (152)
	ANSI 6061-T6	40 (275)	45 (310)
	ANSI 7075-T6	73 (503)	83 (572)
Nickel-Copper	Monel 400	30 (207)	79 (544)
Titanium	RS 140	140 (965)	150 (1,033)
Naval Brass	UNS C46200	53 (365)	75 (517)
Malleable Iron	SAE M3210	32 (220)	50 (345)
Steels	AISI 1018	32 (220)	58 (400)
	AISI 1040	42 (289)	76 (524)
	AISI 304	35 (241)	85 (586)
	AISI 316	35 (241)	85 (586)

* Properties vary widely depending on processing and heat-treatment. Properties for steels are based on hot rolling. Cold-drawn versions of the same grade are work-hardened during the process and have higher strength values. The aluminium strength values are based on their specified temper. The naval brass strength value is based on hardened rod. High-leaded brass is a commonly used alloy and can have a yield strength varying from 17,000 psi to 60,000 psi (117 MPa to 414 MPa) depending on tempering.

Composite Materials

It is a credit to human ingenuity that we could take natural materials and combine them to great effect. Straw and mud were combined to form a simple brick. The ancient Mongolians produced compact, powerful bows by fabricating them out of bone and tendons. Bone was used on the inside, where it would be in compression, and tendons on the outside where the bow was in tension. Natural materials are themselves almost always composites. Rocks, wood, soil and nearly all other natural formations are an intricate mix of materials.

A composite material is considered to be any substance made of two or more different materials. Selecting complementary materials allows material scientists to customise composites for a particular application. Composites are typically understood to be large-scale mixing of materials like the powerful mixture of reinforcing steels in concrete. However, creative use of 'composites' is also used at the molecular level. Polymers and metals are often engineered with additives that add strength, ductility and other desirable characteristics.

Composites used in fabrication generally consist of *fibres* and *resins*. The function of the fibres is to produce strength and stiffness while the function of the resin is to hold the fibres in place. In a more general form, fibres are referred to as *reinforcements* and resins as the *matrix*. There are three classes of composites based on the matrix material. They are referred to as polymer matrix composites (PMC), ceramic matrix composites (CMC) and metal matrix composites (MMC). Polymer matrix composites are used in boat construction because they have a very high strength-to-weight ratio. In addition, they are usually inexpensive and will not corrode.

Composite Terminology

Reinforcement = Fibre = Filament* = fibreglass, carbon, Kevlar, boron, bismaleimide, polyimide, etc.

Matrix = Resin = Thermoset Plastic = polyester, vinylester, epoxy, etc.

* Filaments are produced during manufacturing and are made into *yarns*. Yarns are grouped into *rovings*.

Composite materials, such as *fibre reinforced plastics* (FRP) used in boat construction, are stronger than the individual constituents because the resins are fluid and are able to transfer and distribute stresses among the fibres. There are many terms used for FRPs and it is worthwhile to briefly present them. FRP is synonymous with GRP (glass reinforced plastics) and FRC (fibre reinforced composite). Mouldable plastics containing randomly oriented fibre reinforcements are also sometimes called 'composites' although it is more common to refer to them as reinforced plastics. Some terms are maintained from the era when fibreglass reinforcement was the only option. For example, applying reinforcing tape over a joint or object is still called 'glassing over'. The lay public will call most FRP boats 'fibreglass' for years to come.

Laminates, which are used to construct most boat hulls, consist of two or more layers of reinforcements, or *plies*, bonded by a resin. Many parts of a boat are also made with *sandwich construction*. Sandwich construction is a special type of laminate construction that increases the rigidity and buckling resistance of the laminates.

Strength and stiffness come from two different features. Although a laminate can be very strong, it would not be rigid if it were thin; rather it would behave just like a thin sheet of metal and easily flex and buckle. To make the sheet rigid, stiffening ribs/stringers could be used. Alternately, more plies could be layered to make a thicker laminate. However, this thick laminate would be rigid

and strong but very heavy and expensive. Sandwich construction includes a thick layer of low-density material such as balsa wood, foam, or honeycomb material between the plies. The resulting sandwich composite would be lighter, cheaper and nearly as strong and as rigid as an equally thick laminate. Commercial cores sold under various trade names include end-grained balsa wood, urethane foam, PVC foam, Kevlar honeycomb and aluminium honeycomb. Plywood could be considered a core but is heavy and very strong and rigid on its own. Covering plywood with FRP does improve the strength of the composite but it is more often used to protect the plywood from moisture.

Consider one everyday example of sandwich construction: corrugated cardboard. Corrugated cardboard is made entirely of paper. In the centre of the cardboard, a wavy (corrugated) section of paper separates the outer layers. Consequently, the corrugated

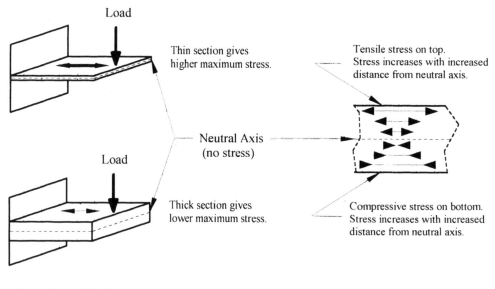

Plates loaded in flexure.

Cross-section of plate showing distribution of stresses when loaded in flexure.

Figure 8   Relationship between stress and thickness

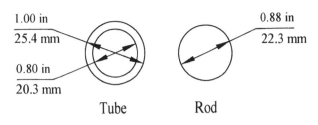

The above tube and rod have the same rigidity; however, the tube is almost one-half the weight of the rod.

The calculation for the moment of inertia for a rod is simply: $3.14 \times R^4/4$. Therefore for every unit increase in radius, the moment of inertia increases four-fold.

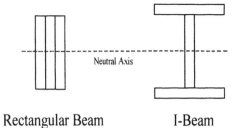

By changing the shape of the rectangular beam to that of an I-beam, as shown above, the rigidity increases by over 75 % yet the weight is unchanged. However this is only true in the vertical plane. In the horizontal plane the I-Beam is 250% less rigid than in the vertical plane. This illustrates that if the direction of loading can be predicted, it is very beneficial to develop a shape that puts as much of the material as far as possible from the neutral axis.

Figure 9   Moment of inertia of different shapes

cardboard is made rigid. Imagine how floppy the cardboard would be if the corrugated section was flattened out and all the paper layers were laid on top of each other. Even if the flattened paper were replaced by steel it would still not be as rigid as the corrugated form. This increased rigidity and strength is only apparent when the corrugated cardboard is bent. In pure tension it has virtually no effect, that is, the flattened paper would be as strong as the corrugated paper if it were pulled at the ends.

These relationships between rigidity and shape are quantified by the *moment of inertia*. In the case of flexural loading (a load that produces only a moment, not an axial or torsional force), the stress produced in the part is inversely proportional to the moment of inertia. The higher the moment of inertia, the lower the stress produced under a given load. If a part is designed so that the material is far away from its centre, or neutral axis, it will have a higher moment of inertia than if all the material is bunched up around the centre. In fact, the moment of inertia increases as a cubic function of the distance of the material from the neutral axis. A tube has a much higher moment of inertia than a solid rod of the same mass because the mass of the tube is located further from the centre. Unlike a tube, an I beam has most of its material located along only one plane. Therefore, it has to be oriented correctly with respect to the intended load to take advantage of its shape.

Reinforcement Characteristics that Affect Composite Strength

1. Fibre Material

Fibre material is the principal indicator of a composite's strength. This importance is reflected by the practice of referring to the composite by its fibre material. Fibre strengths are so impressively high that they are waiting for the resins and designs to catch up to their ability. The principal fibre materials for boat construction are fibreglass, Kevlar and carbon. These materials are sometimes mixed to provide a balance of strength and economy. Fibreglass and Kevlar are a common combination.

47

Fibreglass

The varieties of fibreglass fibres referred to as E-glass and S-glass are the most common structural fibres. E-glass is the 'oldtimer' of the group and is still the most commonly used glass in fibreglass reinforced-plastic. It was originally developed for radar domes where its strength and tolerance of radio transmission were required. S-glass is about 33 per cent stronger and 25 per cent stiffer than E-glass but is more expensive. Both fibres are white when dry and translucent when wetted with resin.

Kevlar

Kevlar fibre was one of the first so-called 'advanced' composites and is much stronger and stiffer than fibreglass. Kevlar is a trade name for an aramid fibre derived from nylon and is famous for its impact resistance. One form of Kevlar (Kevlar 29) is used in bullet-proof vests and like all the Kevlars, is not *notch sensitive*; meaning it has relatively low sensitivity to stress concentrations. It also has excellent energy absorption characteristics and fails in a ductile manner unlike the brittle, glass-like failures that occur in fibreglass and carbon. The only disadvantage of Kevlar's gold-coloured strands is its relatively poor compressive strength.

Kevlar has already been outperformed by carbon but it does have higher impact strength than carbon and does not contribute to galvanic corrosion.

Carbon

Carbon fibre is also considered an advanced composite and, due to its strong molecular bonding, is very strong and rigid. Diamonds are made of pure carbon, and with that sort of potential one can understand why this is a very special material. A diamond is one of the three solid forms of carbon. 'Carbon' and graphite are the other two.

Carbon atoms that form a hexagonal shape are the constituents of both carbon and graphite fibres. When these hexagonal 'plates' are stacked up in perfect alignment, the resulting structure is called graphite. However, when the plates are stacked up in random orientations the structure is called carbon. These tightly bound carbon plates make the filament strong. However, this same characteristic also produces a slippery surface and makes resin bonding difficult.

The mechanical properties of carbon are highly dependent on the nature of the parent material or *precursor*. As a result of this dependency on a specific precursor, there are a variety of carbon fibres each with differences in strength and stiffness. Current carbon-epoxy composites can achieve tensile yield strengths of 150,000 psi (1,034 MPa). Carbon has some other impressive features, such as its strength increases with temperature and it has low thermal expansion.

One of the problems with the black-coloured carbon fibre is that it is highly cathodic and can produce strong galvanic corrosion. Consequently, when metal fasteners are required, they must be made from stainless steels, inconels, or titanium.

Table 11

Performance Comparison of Structural Reinforcements

Characteristic	Fibreglass	Kevlar	Carbon
Tensile strength	Fair	Good	Best
Compressive strength	Good	Poor	Best
Shear strength	Good	Poor	Good
Impact strength	Best	Fair*	Poor
Fatigue strength	Fair	Good	Best
High temp. strength	Good	Poor	Best

* Fibres can be made to be highly impact absorbent during failure.

2. Fibre Orientation

Fibres can be oriented in one, two or three dimensions. The composite made from these different orientations will be strongest in the direction of the fibres. Two-dimensional, or *planar*, fibres are usually woven and are commonly used in hull construction. These weaves can be laid on top of each other in different orientations so that they have nearly equal strength in all planar directions. Fibres may be laid in one direction to reinforce areas where the direction of force is well known. Composites made from one or two-dimensional fibres are much weaker in the direction that pulls the fibres or laminates apart. To offset this interlaminar weakness, three dimensional reinforcements can be used. However, there is a disadvantage to three dimensional orientations. If the three-dimensional reinforcements are woven and made to be nearly as strong as one and two-dimensional reinforcements, they are very expensive. A composite can be made truly isotropic in the same manner that we take for granted in metals by introducing short, randomly oriented fibre reinforcements. However, it is not as strong as one and two-dimensional reinforcements. The introduction of randomly oriented fibres is now very common in mouldable plastics and chopped strand construction.

3. Fibre Length
The length of the fibre affects the strength and rigidity of the composite. Generally, the longer the fibre, the stronger the composite. This makes intuitive sense because the extremely strong fibres bear all the stresses whereas with discontinuous composites, made from short fibres, the resin must carry the load between the fibres. An additional advantage of long, continuous fibres is that they can be more densely packed into the resin than short, discontinuous fibres.

Studies of continuous filament wound hulls on scaled models indicate that large vessels can be manufactured with filament wound hulls. However, this construction approach has not been used because conventional filament winding cannot accommodate hullshaped mandrels of any practical size.

4. Fibre and Resin Bonding
In order to get a good bond between the fibre and the resin a *sizing* is sprayed onto the fibre strands. Sizing is also used to protect the filaments and lubricate them for easier weaving. The composition of the sizing is dependent on the material being used. An important constituent of the sizing used on fibreglass is the *coupling agent*. The coupling agent neutralises the naturally charged state of fibreglass so that it can bond with a neutral resin.

The bonding of the resin to the fibre is very important because the resin must completely encapsulate the fibres to prevent buckling. Voids in the resin leave unsupported, skinny fibres that will easily buckle under compression.

5. Resin
The purpose of the resin is to hold the fibres in place and to deform under stress, thereby allowing the stresses to be distributed to the much stronger fibres. Resins also protect the fibres from abrasion. The resin material is selected based on the fibre material and the temperature range required. Resin development is a dynamic field and, along with the bonding agents, is constantly improving.

Polyester, vinylester and epoxy are common resins used in boat construction. These resins all shrink slightly when cured and they all absorb moisture. Epoxy is better than polyester and vinylester resins because it has stronger fibre adhesion, less water absorption and less shrinkage. It also does not generate noxious volatile organic compounds during processing. As one might suspect, along with all these good characteristics comes a higher cost. Consequently it is usually used only on advanced composites. Vinylester is a newer resin in the ester family and has better bonding than polyester yet is still less expensive than epoxy.

An attractive way to work with resins is to use pre-pregnated fibres or 'pre-pregs'. Pre-pregs are dry materials and are easy to work with. The resin is activated when the pre-preg is heated to over 200°F (93°C).

Connecting Composites

The biggest difficulty of composite construction is connecting them to other materials. The best way to attach two composites is to bond them using overlapping layers. A simplified form of this type of bonding is often used to attach bulkheads to the hull and deck. Typically, fibreglass tape is bonded to the bulkhead and the adjoining hull or deck. Sharp corners need to be avoided at this connection to reduce the stress concentration. This is sometimes accomplished by inserting a small fillet-shaped piece at the junction and taping over it.

Mechanical fasteners can also be used to connect composites. These are commonly used to connect the hull and deck as well as the hull and deck-mounted components. Very strong hull-to-deck connections are produced by bolting the hull and deck together and then covering the joint and fasteners with overlapping FRP.

Great attention must be given to holes because they are a source of stress concentration. Specialised drills have been developed for advanced composites. In very well-designed structures the composite is made more ductile or 'softened' by changing the fibre orientation around the hole.

Critical connections are sometimes made by putting metal inserts into the core of a sandwich panel. Metal brackets that fasten to these inserts connect panels or other objects. 'Tab and slot' connections are another connection scheme currently being investigated. This style of connection has tabs formed into one panel that fit into slots formed in the section to be joined in the same

manner as mortise and tenon joints, long used in wood working. The mortise hole is coated with adhesive to produce the bond. Rabbet joints at the edge of the panel do not work as well as they rely entirely on the adhesive for bonding whereas with the mortise-style the load is carried primarily by the composite panel rather than the adhesive. This joint has proven to be lightweight, inexpensive and very strong yet has not found its way into the boatbuilding field.

Composites versus Metals

Generally, composite materials have the following advantages and disadvantages with respect to metals:

Advantages

  • Higher strength-to-weight ratio
  • Higher stiffness-to-weight ratio
  • Higher fatigue strength
  • Higher impact resistance
  • No corrosion
  • Absorb sound
  • Potential to integrate parts
  • Carbon has natural lubricity

Disadvantages

  • Combustible and produces heavy smoking
  • More complicated manufacturing
  • Advanced composites are more expensive
  • Carbon can produce galvanic corrosion in metals

Fluid Mechanics

Watching the water continually flow past a hull under way, one has to wonder what is really going on down there? Although this is not an issue for the surveyor in the strictest sense, hopefully the surveyor's natural curiosity may be satiated by this brief description of fluid flow and drag.

The study of fluid behaviour is broken down into two disciplines. The first is the study of fluids at rest, called fluid statics. Water's properties at rest provide the basis for buoyancy and stability. The other fluid discipline, fluid dynamics, describes the study of the nature of moving fluids. Fluid dynamics describes the nature of drag and propulsion.

Buoyancy and Stability

The first law of fluid statics states that a fluid contained in a vessel, like water in the ocean, will distribute an external pressure uniformly throughout the fluid. That is, a fluid will not have some portions in compression and others in tension as solids can. This law, referred to as *Pascal's Law*, applies only when the pressure produced by the fluid's weight is neglected.

Water lies flat because the force of gravity is applied uniformly over its surface. If water tries to lift up above the surrounding water, the weight of the elevated water cannot be supported by the surrounding water (specifically, it cannot carry any of the shear stresses.) The water therefore drops down to the same level as the remaining water. The resulting surface is called the free surface and other external forces, besides the earth's unrelenting gravity, can affect it. Wind, of course, is the principal culprit in making waves and the gravitational pull from the sun and moon creates the tides. However, water current, seismic energy, geothermal energy and even surface tension all affect the free surface of the oceans and lakes.

The pressure experienced by a water molecule increases with depth. The molecules below the free surface not only experience the earth's gravitational pull (which is reduced by less than one per cent in the deepest oceans) but all the weight of the water above it. The gravitational pull on all the air above the free surface is small, only 14.7 psi (101 kPa or 1 bar), but the gravitational pull of the denser water molecules is much higher.

Buoyancy

The second law of fluid statics is the famous Archimedes Principle. This principle states that an object placed in a liquid will increase the level of the water until the weight of the water moved up is equal to the weight of the object. The buoyant force created by the water is equal to the weight of the water displaced.

Specifically,

Buoyant Force = Density of Displaced Liquid × Volume of Displaced Liquid.

The actual height of the water displaced is

therefore dependent on the density and the available surface area. Buoyancy simply requires that the overall density of an object be less than water.

Steel will sink in water because the steel is denser than the water. However, a shape fabricated by steel with a core of air (like a boat hull) has an average density much less than water and therefore floats. Water density is not constant however; its density increases with salinity and decreases with temperature. Therefore, as indicated in the buoyancy force equation above, the load-carrying ability of a vessel varies in proportion to the water density.

The practical implication of varying water density is that the maximum load-carrying ability must be altered to reflect the varying buoyancy provided by different seas. Load lines, commonly known as 'marks' or Plimsoll lines (named in honour of the British Parliamentarian Samuel Plimsoll, who spearheaded numerous laws that improved sailor safety), are marked on the side of ship hulls. These lines publicly portray the maximum load and minimum freeboard of the ship. When the appropriate mark sinks to sea level, the ship is full. The lines are usually marked TF (Tropical Fresh Water), F (Fresh Water), T (Tropical), S (Summer), W (Winter), and WNA (Winter North Atlantic) in order of increasing freeboard requirements.

The load required to immerse a boat a given depth is the unit used to describe buoyancy. This value varies with water density and changes to the boat's waterline area with respect to draught. As a vessel is loaded, the waterline area immersed is increased due to bow and stern overhangs and flared freeboard. Therefore, the load required to settle the vessel increases with increasing load.

Stability

Stability is a more complicated concept to quantify. *Webster's Dictionary* defines stability as 'the property of a body that causes it when disturbed from a condition of equilibrium or steady motion to develop forces or moments that restore the original condition'. The 'body' is constantly disturbed on boats. When considering the stability of a boat, the stability must be insured in the chaotic conditions of heavy weather as well as under varying boat loads. Intuitively we know that a low centre of gravity and a wide beam increases a boat's stability. However, both adding weight to lower the centre of gravity and increasing beam reduce a vessel's speed. Consequently, the stabilising forces that only come into serious play under heavy weather have to be measured against vessel performance. Multi-hull vessels avoid the speed penalty of wide-hull beams by using widely spaced slender hulls. In this manner, they achieve a wide effective beam without a speed handicap. Therefore, in the case of sailboats, they can carry more sail and generate more power. In the case of powerboats, they can be built with a much lighter displacement yet still achieve adequate stability.

The point at which the buoyant force acts is called the *centre of buoyancy*, which is located at the centre of gravity of the displaced water. To produce a stable object, the centre of gravity of the object must lie in vertical alignment with the displaced liquid's centre of buoyancy. Vessel stability, in the conventional sense of the term, is defined by the buoyant forces produced by the hull shape that maintain the boat's trim when the centre of gravity and buoyancy move out of vertical alignment. When wave action and other dynamic forces rotate the hull, the shape of the displaced liquid changes and therefore moves the centre of buoyancy. For small angles of heeling, the centre of buoyancy rotates around the *metacentre*. Initial stability increases with increased distance between the metacentre and the centre of gravity. The horizontal distance between the centre of buoyancy and the centre of gravity determines the righting moment (moment is the product of force and the distance over which it acts.) See Figure 10.

A square, broad section is more stable than a round section because, when rotated, the sinking edge of the square hull increases the restorative buoyant force. The further the edge is driven under, the stronger the buoyant force. Furthermore, the wider the beam, the higher the righting moment. A round hull section behaves much like a cylinder. A cylinder has neutral stability and does not produce a force that will rotate it back to a given position; this is seen with floating logs that will readily rotate.

The location of the vessel's centre of gravity is the other contributor to stability. The lower the centre of gravity, the greater the stability. This fact suggests that all heavy machinery and cargo should be kept as low as possible. All topside equipment and structures should be as lightweight as possible. It is for this

reason that designers rush to use lightweight materials for the superstructure and rigging. This sensitivity to elevated weight applies to repair work – it is very tempting to replace an ailing wooden mast with a carbon fibre one.

When a moment is applied anywhere on the boat, it will roll around the centre of floatation. The centre of floatation is the centre of the waterline area. With a rectangular waterline section, the centre of floatation would be in the middle, whereas with a section in which the stern was much wider than the bow, the centre of floatation would be located closer to the stern.

Sailing vessels used to employ internal ballasting. Originally water, rocks and soil (responsible for inadvertently transplanting seeds worldwide) were lowered into the bottom of the sailing vessels. At least as early as 1873, when the 132 ft (40 m) schooner *Mohawk* capsized in a violent squall while at

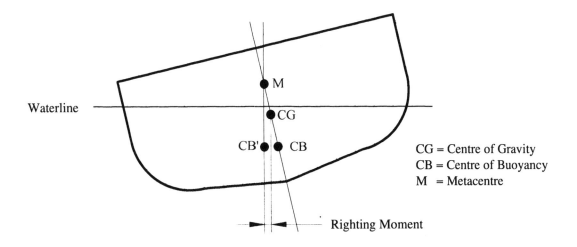

Waterline

CG = Centre of Gravity
CB = Centre of Buoyancy
M = Metacentre

Righting Moment

Because this hull has rotated, a new Centre of Buoyancy (CB') is established. The buoyant force of the hull produces a moment over the horizontal distance between CB' and CG. The Centre of Buoyancy rotates around the Metacentre over small angles

Figure 10   Hull forces

anchor with its sails set in New York Harbor, the problem with shifting internal ballast was recognised. From this time, sailboats gradually started to use external ballast attached underneath the hull. The advantage, as evident by our understanding of stability, is that the external ballast moves the vessel's centre of gravity lower. However, one of the concerns designers had when discussing these matters over 100 years ago was the problem of excessive stability. If a boat were too resistant to wave and wind action, the boat would be heavily stressed, not to mention an uncomfortable ride in beam seas. Moreover, affixing external ballast is no simple matter, and the security of the ballast attachment is still a salient concern for the marine surveyor.

Tankers are faced with an unusual stability consideration because their cargo readily moves. With a constant wave frequency, the fluid would move at the same frequency as the waves. This resonance would easily tip them over. Ingenious solutions have been developed in addition to the straightforward use of baffles and bulkheads. These solutions involve keeping the main tanks completely full and providing smaller expansion tanks (or trunks) to accommodate thermal expansion. By keeping the main tanks completely full at all times, no internal sloshing can occur.

Drag

Total drag is the summation of three types of drag: friction, pressure and wave-making drag. The hull dragging against the water produces friction drag. Reducing wetted surface, smoothing the wetted surface and reducing speed can lower this drag. The pressure drag results from the pressure difference between the front of the hull and the stern, where wake eddies exist. For a given hull length, the amount of drag contributed by pressure drag increases with beam. That is, a slender sculling craft's drag would be nearly all friction drag whereas a beamy barge's drag would be nearly all pressure drag. Much more important than the beam however, is the hull shape. Streamlining of the hull is vitally important in reducing pressure drag. A hull that is in the shape of a box (flat bow and stern) will have 15 times as much drag as a streamlined hull (rounded bow and stern) of the same beam. With a squared-off bow and stern, the bow impacts the water creating a high pressure, and then radically disengages the water at the stern, thereby producing powerful eddies. These eddies result in very low pressure behind the hull. This combination of flat bow and stern features creates a large pressure differential, resulting in pressure drag across the hull. The streamlined hull gently changes the water direction around the bow and therefore decreases the pressure at the bow. More importantly it allows the water to recombine astern, with the minimum of eddies and subsequent low pressure. Therefore, the streamlined hull produces a lower pressure at the bow and a higher pressure at the stern. Consequently, the pressure differential across the hull is much lower creating a lower pressure drag.

One of the factors affecting pressure drag is the separation of the water boundary layer from the hull. Due to molecular interactions between the solid hull and liquid water, they try to find an equilibrium condition. At the actual point of contact they travel at the same speed, that is the water and hull travel as one, however further away from the hull the water gradually retains its original velocity. This transitional area from where the fluid sticks to a moving object to where the fluid is at its original speed is called the boundary layer.

The boundary layer develops thickness as it travels over the length of the hull; however it is small even when fully developed. For example, with a 50 ft (15 m) vessel travelling at six knots, the boundary layer is little more than a 0.15 inches (3.8 mm) near the stern. The drag and boundary layer description provided here are the same for any gaseous or liquid fluid. Air does not produce as much drag as water because it is not as viscous, or resistant to flow. However, areas above the wetted surface, most notably superstructure, should also be streamlined to reduce pressure drag from the air flow.

Two sorts of boundary layers can develop, laminar and turbulent. In water, only small, slow-moving objects have completely laminar boundary layers. For all practical purposes all boats operate with turbulent boundary layers. Turbulence is still a mysterious contortion of a fluid that flails about in unpredictable ways. However, contrary to the pejorative notion of turbulence, turbulent boundary layers are advantageous. A turbulent boundary layer binds better to a flowing object than a laminar boundary layer. This reduces the pressure drag because it decreases the size and strength of the deleterious wake turbulence.

Consider water flowing around a hull with a laminar boundary layer, the boundary layer will remain attached to the hull almost to its widest point. After this point, the boundary layer will not be able to make the turn inwards behind the hull. However, with a turbulent boundary layer, the boundary layer can turn inwardly behind the hull and separate further abaft. In the case of a hull, the actual boundary layer separation point is 120 degrees from the impact point for a turbulent boundary layer, versus only 82 degrees for the laminar boundary layer. What does this mean? With the laminar boundary layer, a large wake is produced with strong eddies. With the turbulent boundary layer, the wake is reduced. Therefore, the pressure drag is greatly decreased. It is for this reason that golf balls are dimpled. The dimples make the surface rougher and trip up the boundary layer into turbulence. The stickier turbulent

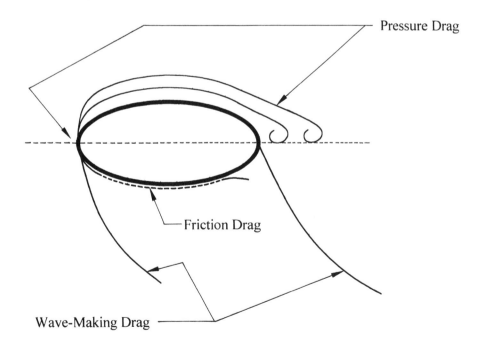

Figure 11   Hull drag forces

layer reduces eddy strength, decreases the pressure drag and therefore provides longer flight. In the case of the golf ball, the increase in friction drag produced by the dimples is more than offset by the decreased pressure drag. Due to their length, any boats travelling above dead slow will always have a turbulent boundary layer; therefore, keeping the hull clean and smooth will decrease the friction drag and is the best way to reduce total drag for a given hull design.

When a hull is forced through the water, separate wave patterns are set up from the bow and stern. Generally, the energy used to make these waves increases in relation to the speed-to-length ratio. As the vessel speed increases, the energy expended in producing bow and stern waves increases rapidly, from being negligible at dead slow speeds to being nearly the entire source of drag on the hull at the maximum hull speed. For large displacement hulls that do not operate near the maximum displacement speed, the operating speed is selected to fall at a speed where the interaction between the bow and stern wave are such that they produce a low wave-making resistance. Wide beams and heavy displacements also tend to produce the highest waves.

Both wave-making and pressure drag are dependent on the speed-to-length ratio and are often combined under the term *residual drag*. This implies that the method of determining this drag value is by subtracting the friction drag from the hull's total drag.

For fast boats, the residual drag can be greatly reduced by decreasing the beam. Decreasing the beam affects stability (and performance in the case of sailboats) so a happy medium has to be obtained. The displacement/length ratio (or D/L ratio) is usually used to describe the effect of displacement on wave-making. The D/L ratio is calculated as follows:

$$D/L = (Displacement) \div 0.01 \times (LWL)^3$$

The higher the D/L ratio the greater the wave-making production of the hull and subsequent resistance. These values start as low as 40 in lightweight racing catamarans and naval destroyers and race upwards to triple digits for workboats.

Checklist and Technique

Checklist and Technique

A marine survey must determine the status of a boat's structure, equipment, mechanical and electrical systems. However, the emphasis of the marine survey must be the investigation of the boat's structure and safety equipment. It may not be practical to inspect all the operating systems; however, the extent of the survey should be agreed upon with the owner prior to the survey. Moreover, the survey report should only comment on systems and equipment actually inspected. An inspection on an unhauled boat is known as a partial survey. The hull structure cannot be evaluated on an unhauled boat; therefore, the boat must be hauled and dry prior to commencing a full survey.

During the survey, consider whether equipment is properly sized. Pay special attention to the sizing of the anchor, rode, mooring lines, cleats and bilge pump. Check the safety equipment against governing regulations. Record the hull identification number, model and operating hours of the engines. Also note the serial numbers of the engines and all fixed electronic and navigation equipment.

Before climbing onto the boat check the supports or cradle, as tipping the boat over would be an expensive and embarrassing event. Most of the support and stability should come from shoring under the chines. Access to the structural features of the boat is critical. In preparation for the survey, pump out any standing bilge water. The lazarettes, lockers, anchor wells and any other areas that allow access to the interior hull need to be emptied of their contents. It is a good safety practice to keep the hatches closed while working on deck, so that while engrossed in some task you do not accidentally step through them.

Try to understand how the loads are carried in the hull and deck as well as by the engine, rigging, rudder, winches and other heavily loaded features. This will provide a good understanding of where problems are likely to originate. The effects of stress concentrations and corrosion will be very important factors in areas of high loading.

Trace the hull and deck reinforcements as much as possible. Inspect the hull where bulkheads or ribs connect, as the hull will see higher loads in these areas. In the same manner, inspect bulkheads where anything running longitudinally butts up against them. This includes partition walls or any other reinforcement that provides longitudinal stiffening. Partition walls or stiffeners of any sort with insufficient doubler plates, butt straps or brackets will create problems when they are not continued through the bulkhead. The unbalanced forces applied to the bulkhead will produce a flexing load on the bulkhead. It is good design practice to maintain all stiffening members, both longitudinal and athwartship, from one side of the hull to the other. This is nearly always done with athwart bulkheads but not with longitudinal stiffeners. Wherever any stiffening member such as bulkheads, ribs, and deck supports are terminated, the member should be blended with a large radius and broadened as much as possible with a doubler plate. In this fashion, the load can be gradually transmitted through the rest of the structure by distributing it over as much area as possible and reducing stress concentrations. Nevertheless, these stiffener terminations are likely areas to develop cracks.

Water weighs 8.3 lb/gallon (1 kg/litre). A deck full of water can easily weigh tons. Moreover, when the water comes in the form of a breaking wave, it also has additional impact energy. Check for buckling of large deck surfaces, especially the forward deck. Planing craft in particular often have weakly reinforced decks. Carefully check their forward decks for damage caused by waves breaking on the deck.

Inspect for cracks of any sort, especially on highly stressed parts such as keel connections, chines, rudders, bollards, cleats, chainplates and stay/shroud terminals. Cracks usually originate in highly loaded areas from a source of stress concentration such as mounting holes and inside corners. A dye penetrant should be used liberally to aid in the identification of small cracks. During the visual inspection, look carefully for cracked welds, crooked or deformed fasteners and corrosion. Also inspect for sharp edges that could cut someone. Hand cuts heal slowly when working on a boat and are especially a nuisance when hands are constantly exposed to seawater.

Look for areas where water can settle, as they are common sources of trouble. This is especially important on the deck, where standing water will rot out wooden super-structures, work its way into a fibreglass core and underneath deck-mounted equipment.

Remember that stainless steel fasteners will galvanically corrode aluminium and, to a lesser extent, brass. Aluminium corrosion will show up as a white flaky material around the stainless steel. Randomly select some fasteners in damp areas or where the potential for galvanic corrosion exists. Inspect them for pitting or crevice corrosion in the threads and head. Tightening of the nut or screw head may reveal dangerous weakening caused by corrosion.

Fasteners work best in shear. The fastened joint is more likely to experience failure when it is in tension. Carefully inspect both the fastener and the material that the fastener passes through. Wood screws and self-tapping screws are especially unreliable in tension. See 'Notes', number 5 for more discussion on this matter.

On sailboats, check the mast step carefully. The mast load needs to be distributed evenly through the keel (or deck with a deck-stepped mast). If the mast butts up against the bottom of the hull, it produces tremendous localised stresses in that area. Support pillars must be broad on all axes to prevent buckling (Try having someone stand on an aluminium can and press the sides of the can in with two sticks. You will see that it hardly takes any force at all to buckle it). Masts that protrude through the deck do not need buckling reinforcements.

As you peer carefully in corners for tiny cracks, look at the big picture also. Once, while inspecting the engine bed of a motor yacht, I started to review the engine layout. I saw something was not right and had to look twice before I realised that the engine block had a long crack along one side. Although not related to safety or structure, this is a very expensive repair and is an example of a problem that stares you in the face so blatantly that you could miss it for the sake of fussy details. I have found many inoperative items that would require expensive repairs that beg to be lost under all the attention given to hull structure and keel attachments. Although everyone has their own approach to inspections, I believe big problems are most easily noticed upon first look. Stand away from the boat and observe it without focusing on anything in particular. Once you get into a

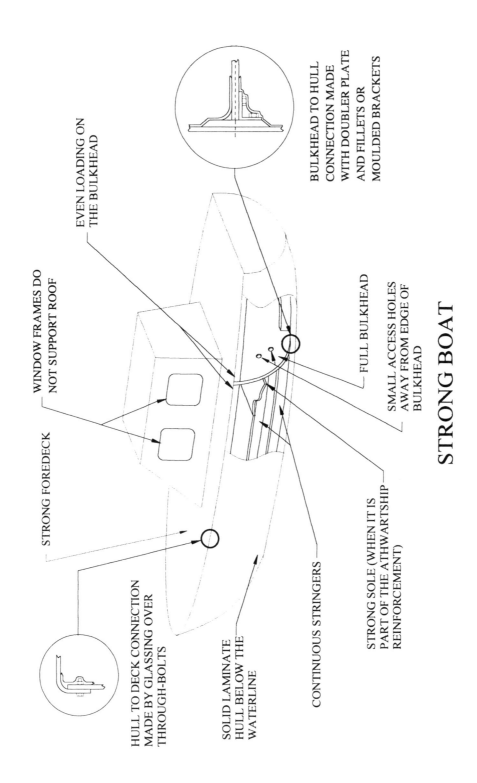

BULKHEAD TO HULL CONNECTION MADE WITH DOUBLER PLATE AND FILLETS OR MOULDED BRACKETS

EVEN LOADING ON THE BULKHEAD

WINDOW FRAMES DO NOT SUPPORT ROOF

FULL BULKHEAD

SMALL ACCESS HOLES AWAY FROM EDGE OF BULKHEAD

STRONG FOREDECK

STRONG BOAT

HULL TO DECK CONNECTION MADE BY GLASSING OVER THROUGH-BOLTS

SOLID LAMINATE HULL BELOW THE WATERLINE

CONTINUOUS STRINGERS

STRONG SOLE (WHEN IT IS PART OF THE ATHWARTSHIP REINFORCEMENT)

61

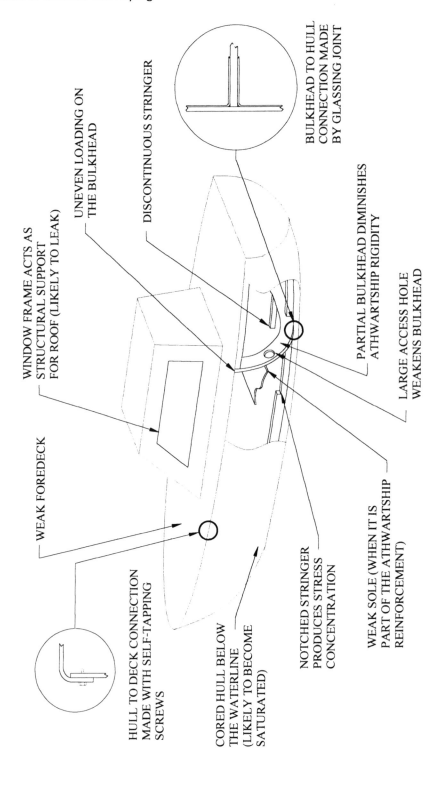

WEAK BOAT

BULKHEAD TO HULL CONNECTION MADE BY GLASSING JOINT

DISCONTINUOUS STRINGER

UNEVEN LOADING ON THE BULKHEAD

WINDOW FRAME ACTS AS STRUCTURAL SUPPORT FOR ROOF (LIKELY TO LEAK)

PARTIAL BULKHEAD DIMINISHES ATHWARTSHIP RIGIDITY

LARGE ACCESS HOLE WEAKENS BULKHEAD

WEAK FOREDECK

NOTCHED STRINGER PRODUCES STRESS CONCENTRATION

WEAK SOLE (WHEN IT IS PART OF THE ATHWARTSHIP REINFORCEMENT)

HULL TO DECK CONNECTION MADE WITH SELF-TAPPING SCREWS

CORED HULL BELOW THE WATERLINE (LIKELY TO BECOME SATURATED)

mode where you look at details the requisite focus, concentration and intensity can prevent you from seeing large-scale problems. Successful surveys rely on intuition along with more scientific underpinnings. Follow your hunches and try to determine root causes of failures.

Consider some sample problems: if deep cracks (beneath the gel coat) radiate in the deck from the starboard pulpit mounting bolts, what might have happened? If the port side is in good condition on both sides of the deck it indicates that the load did not transmit to this side. Even a twisting action on the pulpit would have caused similar cracks on the inside deck surface. Did the starboard side alone get pulled up or did the pulpit flex when a twisting force was applied? Look for signs. Are there cracks or darkened areas in the chrome plating indicating excessive flexing? Because the cracks were caused by tensile and not compressive forces, and assuming the pulpit did not flex thereby preventing the same damage to the port side mountings, the pulpit was obviously pulled up on the starboard side. Therefore, inspect underneath the pulpit for signs of contact. What probably

Do not miss the obvious. This water-cooled exhaust manifold is cracked and will be an expensive repair. Note the tight radius that the water hose makes into the manifold. This feature should be identified in the survey as a potential site for hose cracking.

happened was that an ebbing tide hooked the pulpit on a pier. Assuming this was the root cause (although it could have been caused by other things) look for corroboration. Are there vertical scratches in the hull that may have been produced at the same time? If the vessel is only suspended by the pulpit under an ebbing tide, what else may have occurred? As it was unceremoniously dropped, it may have rolled into the pier causing damage to the hull, bulkheads or other structural elements.

If you found a rusty hose clamp on a potable water hose (stainless steel clamps often use carbon steel worm gears) what might that indicate? Assuming a leaking hose or galvanic corrosion did not cause the rust, it probably indicates that water has travelled down the hose from another point. Trace the hose to see what is happening. Where else would water have migrated after it was finished with the hose clamp? Is the hull-to-deck sealant at fault? Very likely it is a leaking hatch. Track the root cause.

A seacock turns too easily. What has happened? Inspect the stem. Did it corrode through, perhaps due to stray current corrosion, or was it over-torqued when the ball (or gate) seized up due to corrosion? What is the next step? Check all the seacocks thoroughly. If it was stem corrosion, all the plumbing should be suspect because obviously little attention was paid to installing suitable devices.

You see parallel cracks initiated around the after section of a fin keel on a 'U' section hull. The hull shows some deformation where the keel buckled the hull. Suspect keel impact. Look for damage to the keel, especially the lower leading edge. Verifying keel impact would seem easy but one must remember that the damage could have been repaired or covered with fresh paint or be hidden by the mounting blocks it is sitting upon. Inspection of the keel support may also show corresponding damage. A shock that would have caused this hull damage would have placed the afterstay in higher than usual tension so the stay and terminal would have to be checked thoroughly.

A stove's front burner (the one that is most convenient) is clean and shows no sign of being used. It probably does not work. Check it out. Over-cleanliness, tape residue from recently-removed duct tape and fresh paint are not bad things in themselves but should inspire a closer look.

You see acid burns in the battery compartment. Did a battery case rupture or was the boat knocked down in a gale or while being hauled? Look for signs that satisfy you.

The foredeck feels mushy when you jump on it. Is the core saturated, weakly constructed or under-supported below deck? Does the shape change when you jump on it? Check for core saturation by sounding or with a moisture meter. Also remove nearby through bolts and probe the core with an awl to feel for softness. Alternatively, with the owner's permission, drill some probe holes as described in 'Notes', number 1. If the core is not saturated, the sandwich construction or bulkheads are inadequate. What would happen when a wave breaks on the deck? If the deck has been highly loaded by breaking waves it must be checked for damage. The deformation of the deck may have damaged the hull-to-deck connection as well as the hull-to-superstructure connections.

You notice that the lubricator bowl for compressed air line is empty. Advise the owner that it needs to be filled? It is probably not that simple; the bowl was probably never refilled after it was originally set up and all the pneumatic equipment will have experienced high wear.

The starboard genoa track is loose at one end. Assuming the bolt loosened, advise retightening and the application of a thread-locking compound. What happened to the deck when the fastener impacted it with every wave and heave of the sail? Also, what happened to the water that probably leaked through the broken sealant around the loosened fastener? Track the water path, if any, to the bilge.

Survey Format

The goal of a marine survey is to ensure that the boat is safe and identify all existing or potential problems. The first goal is the most important. It is achieved by evaluating the structural integrity and safety equipment. Although a surveyor cannot be expected to vouch for the structural design, fatigue life and performance of a boat, any observations based on experience will be helpful in ensuring safety. A survey report should describe the boat and provide findings on the condition of each system or area. A recommended reporting format includes a title page, vessel data sheet, general description, survey findings and recommendations.

Title Page
Include the client's name, boat name, boat model, location and date of survey, surveyor's name or company.

Vessel Data Sheet
Summary data should be included and contain the following vessel information:

1. Boat name
2. Type
3. Builder
4. Model
5. Hull colour
6. Deck colour
7. LOA (length over all)
8. LWL (length on the waterline)
   Note: Check actual waterline mark based on sediment and discolouration.
9. Beam
10. Draft
11. Displacement
12. Hull number, documentation number, registration number and expiration date.

13. Propulsion engine model and serial number
14. Transmission/drive model and serial number
15. Engine hours
16. Engine fuel type
17. Basic dinghy and trailer information should also be included when required.

General Description

Provide a brief general description of the boat including intended operation. In this section, conditions that limited the survey such as lack of electrical power, engines removed, etc. can be reported. Include a statement of techniques employed during the survey. For example, state that unless otherwise specified, the survey is based on visual inspections and soundings of all reasonably accessible areas.

Survey Findings

The survey report should be divided into sections as indicated on the Survey Checklist (i.e. exterior hull, interior hull, deck, etc.). Each section should start with a general description of the area investigated, which includes material and construction. Following this discussion, report observed problems and conclusions under a subsection entitled 'Findings', wherever possible, a general conclusion of the feature or system's condition. For example, 'The exterior hull is in good condition.' This could be concluded even if there was crazing and small gouges. These problems would, of course, be individually identified in the Findings section. Serious problems would preclude a favourable conclusion on the exterior hull and would be addressed in the Required Repairs section. If no problems are observed, report 'No defects found.'

Recommendations

After the Survey Findings are reported, a Recommendation section should be added. Here, specific courses of action are recommended. This section can be broken down into 1) Essential Repairs, Replacements and Changes; 2) Maintenance Recommendations and 3) Suggested Repairs, Replacements and Changes. The boat manufacturer can be contacted to help with the recommendations.

The *Essential Repairs, Replacements and Changes* sections should list items that must be corrected to ensure that the boat is safe and can operate in the intended manner. Required changes may include rectifying such things as hull and rigging damage that affect structural integrity or missing mandatory emergency equipment and warning labels.

Maintenance Recommendations should highlight items that are most likely to fail, especially those outside the scope of normal maintenance. For example, a kinked or abrading fuel line would be listed here because the survey could identify the part of the hose most likely to fail.

Suggested Repairs, Replacements and Changes can list all minor problems. This section should also include delinquencies in non-mandatory emergency equipment and warning labels.

Miscellaneous

The following should also be included with the survey report:

• A legal disclaimer should be included to cover any liability concerns.

• Signature and date.

• A summary listing of the surveyor's qualifications.

• A package of mounted photographs illustrating specific problems as well as an overview of the boat.

Tools

Non-destructive testing equipment such as that used in radiography, thermography, magnetic particle detection and acoustic emissions are normally unavailable to a marine surveyor; however, the following inspection tools are recommended.

1. A careful eye

An alert visual inspection is the most important survey technique.

2. Hammers

The selection of a sounding hammer is a matter of personal choice. The intent of the hammer is to generate a mechanical sound impulse that will carry through the material. The sound generated will give the ear an idea of the material condition. The process of sounding is explained in detail in 'Notes', number 1.

For FRP, it is important that the hammer does not cause damage; therefore, plastic or soft-face hammers work best. Many surveyors prefer to use the plastic handle of an awl or screwdriver or even a heavy coin.

Hollow sounds produced by tapping a FRP hull and other FRP components will help identify problems. Hammering may also produce rattling that will identify loose assemblies. For metal craft, a metal hammer such as a three-pound (1.8 kg) claw hammer is required. This hammer has a softer head than a ball pein but may still chip coatings. Therefore, plated items should not be struck with a metal hammer. Flat sounds produced by tapping metal parts and sheets may indicate cracks or large-scale corrosion. It is important to use the hammer with great force in areas likely to have corrosion. This hammering will break through paint or filler.

A rubber mallet is helpful in checking mounted components and machinery. The mallet can be swung with considerable force without damaging components or paint.

3. Scratch awl

The handle of an awl can be used to feel for blisters or delamination and can reach crevices that a hammer cannot. In addition, the pick can be used to pry cracks, probe wood and scrape surfaces. The tip of the awl should be filed blunt so that it does not penetrate wood too readily or present a hazard when carrying it. A slotted screwdriver also works well for probing wood.

4. Dye penetrant

A penetrant can be sprayed on suspected areas of cracking. The penetrant will readily identify surface cracks and clearly indicate the extent of damage. The penetrant should not be used on wood and only on FRP when specified by the penetrant manufacturer.

Dye penetrants usually consist of a system of three agents. The first agent is the cleaner. The cleaner is sprayed liberally on the area to be inspected. The cleaner acts on the area for a short time and then is wiped off. The area is resprayed and wiped until it is clean. Unless the manufacturer states otherwise, the cleaner should not be used on FRP. The second step is to spray the clean, dry test area with the penetrant. The penetrant is a coloured chemical that penetrates cracks. The penetrant should be allowed to act for at least five minutes and ideally thirty minutes. The penetrant is then wiped off with a cloth and the cracks will be highlighted by penetrant remaining in the cracks. However, a developer can be sprayed that will make the crack identification easier. Typically, a thin film of developer is sprayed on the test area and allowed to work for five minutes. This will draw out the penetrant and make it stand out very clearly against the developer's white background. The penetrant and developer can be removed after the inspection with the cleaner.

5. *Ohmmeter and extension clip leads*
An ohmmeter is required to check for electrical resistance in the fuel system grounding. An ohmmeter with an audible continuity indicator, that is, the meter produces a sound when continuity is measured, is a great convenience. The clip leads can be attached to the probe leads to give the ohmmeter greater reach and allow it to be clamped to a ground point. Multimeters contain an ohmmeter function.

6. *Magnifying glass*

7. *Mirror with extension handle*
Allows inspection of hard to reach areas.

8. *Flashlight and fluorescent drop light*
Battery-powered fluorescent lights are available that will evenly illuminate an area. Flashlights are good for getting strong light on a small area.

9. *Hand tools*
This selection will vary based on personal preferences but should include at least a socket set, open-end wrenches, a cordless electric screwdriver and pliers. A torque wrench is the correct tool to use when retightening hardware. Although it is always good practice to use a torque wrench it is not essential for non-critical components. An experienced arm is a good torque wrench in most cases; however, for critical connections such as bolts used on structural elements such as the keel, frames and bulkheads, a torque wrench is imperative. The surveyor should not normally be removing these fasteners. Miscellaneous brass and stainless steel hardware should also be kept

on hand to replace items that are accidentally dropped and lost. A tube of silicone sealant should also be included to reseal mounted components that are disturbed.

10. *Scrapers, wire brush, cleaning solvent, rags and paper towels*
Required to prepare areas for inspection.

11. *Chalk*
Outline damaged areas to aid in photographic recording. Lumber crayons may also be used although chalk is easier to remove.

12. *Camera*
To document findings.

13. *Notebook or dictaphone*
To record findings.

14. *Ladder*

15. *Survey checklist*

Other tools are helpful in conducting a survey. For example, a tape measure can be used to measure approximate hull dimensions. Vernier callipers or micrometers are needed to get accurate measurements of material thickness.

An ultrasonic metal thickness sensor is required to do a thorough evaluation of a steel hull. Ultrasonic thickness gauges are also available for FRP. A moisture sensor, copper sulphate solution or magnetic plating gauge to check for the presence of coatings on steel or iron and a magnet to identify metals may also be helpful. A soapy water solution of the sort used for making bubbles is needed to test for gas leaks. Personal gear to consider are such things as hardhats, work gloves, coveralls and a toolbelt.

Survey Checklist

Follow and mark the attached *Checklist* as you work your way through the boat to ensure all items are specifically inspected. Tips and techniques are offered in the referenced annotation in 'Notes'.

Exterior Hull
___ Material condition (1)
___ Through-hull fittings, external (2)
___ Transducers (2)
___ Ground plates (2)
___ Sacrificial anodes (3)

Deck
___ Material condition (1)
___ Hull-to-deck connection (4)
___ Deck hardware (5)
___ Grab rails (6)
___ Toe rails (7)
___ Stanchions (8)
___ Lifelines (8)
___ Scuppers (9)
___ Hatches, external (10)

Bridge/Cockpit
___ Material condition (1)
___ Engine controls

___ Steering
___ Scuppers (9)
___ Antennas
___ Windshield wipers

Superstructure
___ Windows, external (10)
___ Hatches, external (10)

Interior Hull
___ Material condition (1)
___ General condition (e.g. ventilation, leakage, furnishings, doors, cabinetry)
___ Bulkheads/Frames (11)
___ Bilge
___ Sole
___ Through-hulls, internal (2)
___ Backing plates (5)
___ Windows, internal (10)
___ Hatches, internal (10)
___ Bilge pumps (12)

Steering and Propulsion
___ Cables and sheaves/hydraulics (13, 14)
___ Propellers (15)

___ Propeller clearance (15)

___ Propeller shafts (16)

___ Struts (1)

___ Rudders (1,17)

___ Rudder bearings (17)

___ Skegs (1)

___ Trim tabs (17)

___ Emergency steering

Engine Compartment

___ Stringers/engine beds (18)

___ Through-hulls, internal (2)

___ Hoses

___ Valves

___ Ventilation

___ Fire extinguishing system

Engine

___ Installation (e.g. coolant, air intake and exhaust) (19,20)

___ General condition (e.g. damage, overheating, leakage, belts, starting system)

___ Engine mounts

___ Operation (only done as part of a sea trial)

___ Engine mechanic's inspection (21)

Fuel System (19, 22)

___ Mounting

___ Electrical bonding

___ Hoses

___ Valves

___ Fuel tank capacity

Ground Tackle and Cordage (23)

___ Anchors

___ Shackles

___ Chains

___ Rodes

___ Lines

Fresh Water System (19, 24)

___ Capacity

___ Location of tanks

___ Hoses

___ Valves

___ Pumps

___ Taps and sinks

___ Shower

Sanitation System (19, 24)

___ Toilets

___ Hoses

___ Valves

___ Waste pumps

___ Holding tanks

Cooking Gas System (19)

___ Stove/oven (25)

___ Hoses

___ Valves

___ Solenoids

___ Leakage (26)

Freezer/Refrigerator/Air Conditioner (19, 27)

___

Heating System (19)
____ Heaters (exhaust obstruction and heat damage)

____ Hoses

____ Valves

____ Leakage (26)

Canvas (28)
____

Electrical System (29)
____ Shore power

____ Ship power

____ Battery mounting

____ Wiring

Electrical Equipment (19)
____ Lights, internal and external

____ Blowers

____ Fans

Navigation Equipment (30)
____

Radio Equipment (31)
____

Emergency Equipment and Warning Labels (32)
____

Crew Safety and Ergonomics (33)
____

Additional Inspections for Sailboats

Hull /Deck
____ Mast steps (1)

____ Winch mountings (1, 5)

____ Chain plates (1, 5)

____ Keel (34)

Mast/Boom (5, 35)
____ Straightness

____ Spreaders (32)

____ Pins

____ Halyard exits (sharp edges)

____ Antennas

____ Anemometer

____ Wind vane

____ Masthead fly

Stays/Shrouds
____ Wire cable condition (36)

____ Terminals (36)

____ Turnbuckles

____ Clevis pins

____ Chainplates

____ Tangs

____ Adjustable backstay (13)

Whisker Pole/Spinnaker Pole/Traveller/Boom Vang (5)
____ Straightness

____ Pins

____ Shackles

____ Line exits (sharp edges)

____ Traveller car

____ Hydraulic vang (13)

Running Rigging
____ Halyards (14)

___ Wire-to-rope splices

___ Shackles

___ Sheets

___ Furling gear

___ Rigging eyes

Sails (37)

___ Sail-cloth condition

___ Reinforcements condition

___ Cringles

___ Battens

Excellent visibility is afforded from this pilot house. Wipers, lights and radar keep the skipper well informed

Notes

1.

FRP

The material condition of fibre reinforced plastic (FRP) can be assessed with a keen eye and sensitive ear. The outside surface should be very smooth and have a glossy sheen as a result of the gel coat finish. Gel coat is a resin applied to the outside of the hull to seal the fibreglass and provide a smooth finish. During manufacturing, gel coat is actually applied to the inside of the mould and the FRP is applied on top of it. There should be no weave pattern or waviness visible on the outside of the hull. Manufacturers finish the inside of the hull and deck in different ways. Regardless of the finish, the inside surfaces should have a shine indicating resin coverage of the fibres although visible fibres are acceptable.

The biggest problem with FRP construction is core adhesion to the surrounding laminates. This has been a chronic and dangerous problem in FRP boats. FRP builders became too optimistic about the core bond strength and their ability to prevent water from getting to the core. Some boats have been built with entirely cored hulls, meaning that the bottom of the hull was also cored. This practice did not work well because the core would eventually get saturated.

Normal hull flexing puts coring that is located in curved sections under high tensile and shear loading. The loads are produced because of the different movements of the inner and outer laminate. When the hull flexes, the inner or outer laminate will try to move different amounts. Not only can this action cause the core to separate from the laminate, it can actually grind the core away. Therefore, curved sections of sandwich construction need to be inspected carefully.

Try to inspect as much of the hull surface as possible. Although antifouling paint will hide areas, sounding the hull (discussed later) and randomly removing some of the antifouling paint will help reveal the hull condition.

It is important to distinguish between minor gel coat cracking and structural problems in FRP. Small cracks and gouges in lightly loaded areas are acceptable in terms of structural integrity. However, these defects may allow water into the laminates. Water, where it does not belong, will eventually cause problems in anything. In the case of laminates, the expansive force of freezing water will further drive apart the laminates. Some core materials will be softened by long-term water saturation. Although small cracks may eventually permit larger problems, large cracks or cracks in heavily loaded areas need to be repaired immediately. Cracks weaken a section by reducing the area over which a load may be distributed, thereby increasing the section's stress. The ends of a crack produce stress concentrations because of the rapid change in shape introduced into the material.

The surveyor should advise the client that all cracks be sealed to prevent water penetration. Moreover, the surveyor should

72

recommend a course of action for dealing with cracks and advise whether the cracks should be merely monitored or repaired. Deep cracks and those located near highly stressed areas must be repaired. Keep in mind that cracks can easily be hidden, and maybe maliciously so, by paint. Fortunately, the cracks in the gel coat give clues as to where deeper laminate cracks may reside. Common gel coat cracking patterns include parallel cracks, star-shaped cracks, crazing and blistering.

Parallel cracks indicate overflexing of the gel coat and sometimes the underlying laminate. This is usually due to insufficient stiffness in the affected section and is a common problem in sections with 90-degree bends and no bracing. Special attention must be given to chines or other sharp corners in the hull, deck, superstructure, bridge and cockpit. These areas will show the first signs of boat damage because of stress concentrations and exaggerated flexure at their corners. If the stanchions or rubrails are damaged, there has probably been a collision of some sort. As a result, damage to the hull and framework should be suspected.

The use of one-piece moulded fibreglass liners is a common method of producing interiors. These liners work well in keeping water out of the crevices produced in more traditional joinery. The only disadvantage of the one-piece liners is that they often develop cracks on inside corners where the gel coat could not bind to the laminate. Liners may also produce parallel cracks due to the exaggerated flexure in the corners.

Star cracks (cracks radiating outwards from a small area) are caused by a point impact at the centre of the star. Crazing is a dense pattern of small surface cracks. An overly thick gel coat layer usually causes crazing. However, crazing over a small area may also be caused by deep blistering or some other subsurface defect.

Osmotic blistering shows up as small bubbles contained by a thin layer of material. The blisters are caused by water migrating through the outer FRP layers, dissolving the subsurface resin. Water-soluble chemicals are used during hull construction and if they are not correctly blended and smoothed out, an osmotic pressure develops between the outside water and the soluble chemicals. This pressure allows water to move into the FRP and separate the laminates. Sealants such as urethane/silicone paints or epoxies and other barriers are used in many boats to produce an impervious water seal on the hull and prevent osmotic blistering.

To determine crack depth and its effect on the boat's structure, FRP cracks should be inspected as follows:

1. Probe the crack to get an idea of its depth. Use an awl to pry into the crack. Inspecting with the assistance of a flashlight and magnifying glass will allow better visibility. An appropriate die penetrant may be used to determine the length of cracks in critical areas.

2. Inspect the cracked area from the opposite side. Look for cracking or discoloured lines that match the gel coat. This area should also be probed with an awl handle to reveal any cracking. These signs indicate deep or penetrating cracking.

3. Push against cracked and uncracked areas of similar shape. For example, if a section of the starboard coaming has a crack, check the port side in the same area. Observe whether the cracked section is more flexible than the uncracked section. If it is, the crack deeply penetrates the laminate.

4. Sounding the cracked area and comparing it to the uncracked area may produce a different sound. This procedure is described in further detail below.

FRP (as well as wood) problems can be detected by sounding the material. Sounding is simply tapping on the material and listening for sound characteristics. This requires a plastic hammer or awl handle and a little experience. Generally, uncored FRP will generate a high-pitched ring when struck, whereas a delaminated section will produce a much lower pitched hollow sound. Cored laminates will produce a lower-pitched 'thud' sound than uncored laminate when struck hard. The key to using soundings is to listen for differences between good and suspected 'bad' sounds. Sounding will detect incongruities such as delaminations and deep cracks. In a suspicious area, use the palm of one's hand or awl handle to feel the resistance of the material. In this manner, one can get a feel for whether the unusual sounding is due to delamination, or the separation of the sandwich core. If the surface deflects very easily then stiffens, you are probably feeling delamination. On the other hand, if the surface deflects with moderate pressure and then stiffens, it is probably core separation. Needless to say, soundings are completely ineffectual and actually deceptive at temperatures below freezing. Water is likely to freeze in any voids and make them sound as if they are solid.

The deck, which is usually of sandwich construction, can be tested by walking on it and feeling for 'mushiness' or excessive deflection underfoot. A mushy deck is an indication that the core has softened (frequently due to water saturation) or in generally poor condition. If core separation is felt, drill a probing hole into the suspected area. Look at the core shavings coming from the drill bit and feel for moisture. Drilling will require the owner's permission. However, the normal technique to reattach dry coring is to drill a series of holes in the delaminated section and squeeze epoxy into the void. Therefore, drilling is required to produce the repair and the probe hole will be one of the many required. If the core material is wet, as often occurs around overstressed or poorly sealed deck hardware, the coring needs to be cut out and reattached.

This involves cutting out the laminate and chiselling the damaged coring out. This is a major repair operation and will make the probe hole inconsequential. If permission to drill a probe hole cannot be secured, the core and its bonding to the laminate can be determined by removing bolts from various non-critical deck-mounted components. Do not remove the deck-mounted component if possible as that will disturb the seal. Probe the deck through holes with an awl or stiff wire and check for water damage, cracking or separation. When reattaching the bolts, apply silicone into the top of the hole. The sealant will squeeze out under the pressure of tightened bolts and provide additional sealing between the deck-mounted component and the deck. If the component is removed, check the integrity of the gasket or sealant. Repair the sealant as necessary.

Moisture meters can be very helpful in identifying saturated plywood or other coring material. They should be used on encapsulated plywood and cored surfaces to determine the approximate moisture content. They are a beneficial adjunct to the more direct methods of sounding, probing and test drilling. It is important to note that moisture meters are not reliable at temperatures near or below freezing.

An awl handle should be pressed against the hull to feel for blistering or other signs of delamination. The area around the chain plates and other highly stressed sections should be checked carefully.

Although rarely requested, the best way to determine the condition of FRP and core material is to extract a sample. The sample will clearly show any core saturation and delamination. A sample hole needs to be cut from the outside of the hull at a slow feed with a sharp, lubricated hole cutter. In the case of hull samples, the samples should be taken at several points, especially below the chine. It is best to get the recommendations of the designer or manufacturer in identifying check points (and procedures for the subsequent repair of the holes).

If a sample is taken, it can be sent to a laboratory for evaluation. The specific test requirements and approximate material thickness should be determined prior to contacting the laboratory. If the boat is built to a classing society's scantlings rules, they will have specified the thickness of the hull, frame and other structural requirements. The laboratory can then specify their sample size requirements. The testing laboratory will cut the sample and prepare beams for microscopic and mechanical evaluations. These tests can include tensile, compressive, flexural, interlaminar and short beam shear strengths. The samples can then be dissolved to obtain a fibre/resin ratio and void content.

However, if a sample of the FRP is available due to the installation of a through-hull and laboratory tests are not required, the edge of the sample can be studied. Look for material problems such as voids, blobs of resin, varying ply thickness, low reinforcement density, changes in resin colouration or crystal size. If the resin is sticky, it probably means that the resin is uncured and that insufficient resin hardener was used or was not mixed thoroughly. Air bubbles can be caused by poor resin mixing technique and insufficient squeegeeing. These casual observations can only be considered a problem if they differ greatly from other sections of the hull or from past experience with the same boat model.

Liners are sometimes combined with the structural supports for the hull. This grid/liner contains the stringers and athwart reinforcements that on FRP boats were traditionally constructed with plywood-cored fibreglass. The significant problem with these integrated grid/liners is that they are largely inaccessible for inspection. It is very unfortunate that inspection ports are not provided on these designs. The best way to judge the bonding of the grid where visual inspection cannot be done is to heavily strike the outside of the hull,

under the liner, to try to listen for the separate movement of the grid/liner. (See also 'Notes', number 11.)

Steel and Aluminium

Steel and aluminium hulls should be inspected vigorously for corrosion. Corrosion will often be hidden by paint or lie in obscured areas. Liberally sound the hull and structural members. Wearing earplugs will make this procedure more comfortable. Corrosion nearly always exists on steel boats; therefore, an awl must be used to inspect suspicious painted areas such as those showing bubbles, discolouration or moisture. Critical structural members and connections must be chipped free of paint and scale then cleaned with a solvent prior to inspection.

An ultrasonic thickness gauge can be used to determine the metal thickness. The gauge must be closely coupled to the metal and one must be on guard for inaccurate readings. Ultrasonic gauges will occasionally give false readings due to multiple reflections or when working through a rough surface. The measured section must be free of corrosion, scale or loose paint. Moreover, the thickness of the plate should be measured by calipers and compared to the measurement provided by the ultrasonic gauge. This corroboration will ensure that the gauge is providing measurements in the correct order of magnitude. Multiple reflection will be obviously too high for the subject panel. Still, some experience is required to use them reliably.

Cracks and corrosion often develop at welded joints and therefore require close inspection. When dissimilar metals are welded together, the weld may draw away from one of the metals. If a normal, high carbon stainless steel is used for filler, it will have very poor corrosion resistance. This is also true for the stainless steel in the heat-affected area. Low carbon forms of stainless steel such as AISI 304L/BS 304S11 and AISI 316L/BS 316S11 are made specifically for high temperature applications. Rivets can be attacked by corrosion, deformed by time or have their heads nearly removed by sandblasting or descaling.

Cracking in metals is unusual and unacceptable – not to be confused with cracks in FRP which may not be serious. Cracks should be inspected with the aid of a die penetrant to reveal the full extent of the crack. A long hairline crack may be found which extends much further than the crack that was identified by eye. A cluster of irregular cracks is particularly problematic because it indicates intergranular corrosion or metallurgical problems. As described previously, welds are the most likely features to show cracking and corrosion. The cracking may in fact be a partial separation of the weld, or perhaps was evidence of an incomplete weld. These weld fissures need to be carefully cleaned and probed to determine if there is separation or a through-crack. Cast irons may show scaling but these will flake off and are usually inconsequential. Aluminium, stainless steel and other corrosion resistant metals are subject to pitting and crevice corrosion. Although this corrosion can be identified visually, the extent of damage done by these forms of corrosion cannot be determined visually.

Wood

Wood is a beautiful and forgiving material. Wooden hulls afford a quiet and pleasing ride. However, wooden hulls spend their days swelling, contracting and fighting decay. Wooden boats need a lot of maintenance; constant painting or varnishing is required to keep them sound. Wooden structures gradually change their shape by the 'working' action of wood wearing against wood, and by natural sagging of wood under continuous load. 'Hogging' of the keel is caused by the stem and stern gradually drooping below the midsection because of the relative differences in their buoyancy*. For these reasons, wooden boats must be sighted carefully to check their shape. Looking down the hull from both the bow and stern, check for twisting, bulging or any other condition that indicates that the hull shape has deformed. The keel must be straight, although setting the weight of the hull on the keel when hauled will usually force it to be straight. Forcing the hull to rapidly return to its correct shape may create separation of the hull to deck joint sealant or cracks in the paint. Although sighting down the hull is critical for wooden boats, sighting should be conducted regardless of the material. Sightings will ensure that all underwater appendages, most critically keels on sailboats, lie longitudinally on the centreline. A canted keel slows the boat and places a continual torsional force on the hull. Bilge keels, of course, will not lie on the centreline yet they must lie parallel.

Wood is deceptively resilient. Wooden structural members can be cracked, rotted and in horrible condition, yet serve their intended function very well.

The principal issues on wooden boats are 1) wood cracking, 2) wood decay and 3) fastener conditions. Wooden boats will eventually need to have every part replaced. Normally individual frame sections and planks are replaced as needed until the condition of the entire boat is so decrepit that it is scrapped. The first part of the hull inspection should be to inspect the frames and planks for cracking, rot or other damage. Cracked or rotted frames and split-edged planks are unacceptable and need to be replaced immediately.

One should assume at the outset that there is rot in a wooden boat and work diligently to find it. Rot will hold paint well, and this is a common method of covering this problem. Sounding the wood is the fastest way to

---

* Hogging is also the term used to describe the loads experienced by the boat when a wave's crest is amidships. Sagging is the opposite load. That is the wave crests lie at the bow and stern. This hogging and sagging put opposite stresses on the hull.

evaluate a large area. Rot will produce a dull thud. However, the wood should also be probed with an awl or slotted screwdriver at various points to better detect rotting. Discolouration or lifting paint is an indication of rot. Inspection points should focus on areas where water accumulates. This includes the top surface of flat members, such as the top of the deck beams, keel and garboard areas. Signs of water are indicated not only by staining and moisture but also by cupped planks, shifted scarf joints, discolouration and a fuzzy surface texture. Other common areas for rot include overlapping wood such as around stringers and ribs, butt joints, hull-to-deck connections, under-deck hardware, the bottom of vertical sections of the super-structure, windows and fasteners. Cracks or checks in the wood will hold water and can cause deep rot.

Although rot is the biggest problem normally encountered in wooden boats, check for delamination in plywood resulting from adhesive degradation. Sometimes non-marine grades sneak into production.

Antifouling paint does a good job of protecting wood from worms and marine growth. However, look for areas that are missing this protection and investigate them carefully for worm damage. Worm damage usually does not produce rot's discolouration or extreme softening of the wood. The most obvious method to find worm infestation is to shave down the wood and look for their long channels in the exposed wood. However, a less invasive approach is to look for water weeping from the worms' entrance holes.

When wooden fasteners loosen they can free planks to jut out and allow other movements, including the loosening of a ballast keel. Protruding planks is a relatively common problem in wooden boats and is usually caused by fastener corrosion or localised rotting. Occasionally, fasteners can also simply back out due to boat movement and vibrations. The plank-to-frame connection must be tight. Pry underneath the plank with a screwdriver and try to force the plank away. The plank should hold firm under this pressure. The plank-to-frame connection is the most common area for fasteners to waste because this junction holds moisture. The expansion of steel fasteners as they rust can also cause wood to split. A wooden boat that shows bleeding rust signs needs to be refastened at the very least.

To evaluate fastener-related problems, remove some of the plank fasteners, inspect the fasteners and probe the holes. Rescrew the fasteners and feel how well they tighten into the wood. If a fastener is very difficult to get

A wooden boat at the end of its line. The stem is cracked and dislocated. The lower planks are rotted. Note that the planks are nailed. Nails are notoriously unreliable fasteners.

out, leave it alone. Fasteners that are in wet or heavily loaded areas should be inspected first. Check the keel and garboard as well as under the engine and tanks.

Keels

Keels often take a pounding. They bear the brunt of the vessel's contact with mother earth during haulings and groundings. Regardless of the material, the bottom of the keel needs to be inspected carefully. This can be a very frustrating exercise because the mounting blocks prevent easy inspection. Visually inspect all accessible areas. Where blocks prevent inspection, inspect the area above the blocks for any indication of

This hull was not designed to carry the loads produced by the keel. Note the parallel cracks in the FRP that indicate over-flexing. The keel is obviously pulling free. Because the hull's keel support is inadequate, these problems cannot be fixed by simply replacing the keel bolts.

The damage done by grounding can be extensive. The damage done to the hull in the after section of the fin keel needs to be thoroughly investigated from inside. Fortunately, this boat did not have an integral liner/grid.

damage. This might show as a deformation, radiating cracks or abnormal paint appearance. Also look for parallel cracks where the keel attaches to the hull. If there is damage to the bottom of the keel, remember that the force that caused the damage will have transmitted through the hull and its ramifications need to be carefully addressed. This includes the keel connection and the afterstay along with its corresponding chain plates.

2.

The thought of having holes on the bottom of a boat should rightfully be a concern. Consequently, through-hull connections are a critical check on a survey. If anything associated with the through-hull fails (e.g. sealant, fairing block, transducer, valve, hose or surrounding hull material) the boat will take on water and possibly sink. Visually inspect the inside and outside of the through-hulls and look for looseness, cracks, leakage and corrosion. All through-hulls (except for transducers) should be tapped with a rubber mallet prior to inspection to reveal any problems.

There are several types of valves used as seacocks. A seacock is only needed to function in a fully opened or fully closed condition, therefore efficient, low cost valves such as ball, gate and plug valves are commonly used. These valves are recommended for applications where they are either fully open or fully closed. Throttling, or partial opening of these valves causes them to wear quickly. Ball valves, which are probably the most durable seacocks, work by rotating a ball with a hole in it. When the hole is lined up between the valve body inlets, it is open, when turned perpendicular it is closed. The best valves are made with a bronze body and stainless steel ball. The only disadvantage of these valves is that they require a lot of torque to rotate the ball. However, this is easily overcome with a long handle. Gate valves are also used although they are generally not as

durable in seawater applications. Gate and plug valves work by driving a gate down into the valve body to stop flow. Opening the gate allows for flow.

Check seacocks for operation. If a valve turns very easily, the stem may be corroded through. To inspect the valve, remove the hose and watch it operate. Tapered wooden plugs are commonly tied near the through-hull in the event that the valve is sheared off or fails in the open position. The plug can be hammered into the through-hull to stop the flow. A better, more universal backup sealing method is to use expandable pipe plugs. These plugs are an assembly composed of rubber sandwiched between two metal plates. These metal plates are forced together by tightening a bolt that runs through the assembly. This tightening action squeezes out the rubber and produces the seal. The seal is inserted into the pipe, hose, valve, etc. and tightened. The extruded rubber will conform to uneven shapes and produces only gentle, radial forces, not the high longitudinal and radial forces of a tapered plug. Tapered plugs do not work well in cut hose and may actually crack valve bodies or hulls.

Although stating that all hoses must be double clamped may be tiresome, it is still a good practice in that it is cheap, partial insurance against the disastrous consequences of a clamp failure. Many stainless steel band clamps use carbon steel worm gears inside so they are not impervious to corrosion. The best method of attaching fittings or valves to hoses is to use stainless steel bands. The fitting is inserted into the hose and the band is tightened and crimped. However, the significant disadvantage of this connection is that it cannot be assembled and disassembled with hand tools.

Depth and speed transducers as well as grounding plates must also be carefully inspected to ensure that they are well sealed and firmly attached. Check that the fairing blocks and sealants are in good condition.

Check for any hull cracks that may be propagating from the through-hull.

It is worth noting whether the depth sounder is correctly positioned. The manufacturer will offer preferred locations but generally the depth sounder needs to be located so it is fully immersed in smooth flowing, unaerated water. Therefore they are normally located abaft amidships. The sound transmitted by the depth sounder expands as it travels, therefore in the case of sailboats, it must be far enough from the keel so that it does not block the signal and give a false reading.

3.

Sacrificial anodes provide the most common form of protection against galvanic corrosion. However, the types of metals and their relationship in the galvanic series dictate the amount of cathodic protection required for a boat. The boat speed along with fresh or salt water operation also affect cathodic protection requirements. Corrosion protection is considered in the boat design and most recreational boats use zinc anodes. Generally, one sq inch (6.5 sq cm) of zinc anode will protect 250 sq inches (23 sq metres) of steel or aluminium and 100 sq inches (9.3 sq meters) of brass or bronze.

Zinc anodes usually contain aluminium to add strength. Manufacturers will also include trace amounts of materials such as magnesium, copper and cadmium. Consequently, the life and appearance of anodes will vary depending on the composition. Undesirable elements such as iron greatly reduce the effectiveness of the anode; therefore high quality anodes should be used.

The only way to test the condition of the anodes is to conduct a voltage measurement as described by various standards (e.g. American Boat and Yacht Council Standard E-2). However, the anode manufacturer will have recommendations on how to determine the useful life of the anode. Given no other

guidance, the anodes should be replaced when they are halfway dissolved.

If underwater corrosion is occurring near a zinc anode, use an ohmmeter to confirm that the anode is electrically bonded to the surface it is intended to protect. Too many anodes below water can possibly produce overprotection (as well as high drag) that will produce a basic solution in stagnant water. A basic solution can damage aluminium and wood.

4.

Several types of hull-to-deck connections are used in boat construction. The inward turning hull flange is usually the strongest because it is the most protected. A connection made by glassing-over stainless steel through bolts is usually the strongest hull-to-deck connection found in boat construction. This involves running stainless steel bolts through the hull and deck flange. The joint, including the bolts, is then joined by overlapping FRP. When viewed from inside, small bumps will appear in the glassed-over joint where the bolt shafts and nuts are located. The glassed-over fasteners cannot be inspected but one can still look for evidence of water penetration (staining, bubbles, etc.) or FRP peeling at the joint.

Most other designs are lesser variants of the glassed-over through bolts. Self-tapping screws are commonly used. With this attachment method, an aluminium, stainless steel or hardwood backing plate on the inside of the hull should be used as it will hold thread shapes better than FRP. The weakest connection technique is to use pop rivets or screws without a backing plate.

Regardless of the design, if the fasteners are not glassed over, inspect some of them to ensure they are tight and free of corrosion. This will often require the removal of a section of rubrail or inside liner. If possible, spray the connection with a water hose (See 'Notes', number 10). This will assist in identifying any leaks in the hull-to-deck sealant. Inspect the entire length of the connection to ensure that no separation exists between the hull and deck. Where possible, probe and inspect the sealant to ensure it is pliable and continuous.

Getting a large deck to accurately fit on a large hull is a daunting task. Check the fit up between the hull and deck. A frequently encountered problem occurs when the deck edge flange is forced over a hull that is slightly too large. This force-fit may eventually produce a crack in the flange.

Some small boats are manufactured as monolithic structures by rotational moulding. From a strength standpoint, this is a wonderful technique as the full strength of plastics is used throughout, without the weak point of the hull-to-deck connection. However, sharp corners are still a problem in terms of stress concentration and inherent moulding problems. Other FRP connection methods are described in the 'Primer on Composite Materials'.

5.

All mounted components must be inspected for mechanical integrity, correct operation and secure attachment. These components typically include: cleats, bollards, blocks, sheaves, winches, chain plates, cam cleats, sheet stoppers, tracks, windlasses and deck plates. Tap these components with either a hammer or a rubber mallet and look for rigid mounting and listen to any unusual sounds. Inspect the fasteners, backing plates and washers. Look for any cracking or deformation.

One need not worry too much about fasteners that only carry shearing forces, such as with winches. In the case of shear loading, assuming the load bearing structure is strong, the problems that could be experienced are corrosion and, on a bolted joint, the backing off of the nut. If the hole through which a fastener in shear will pass is located too close to the edge of a material, the fastener could tear out the material when the shear load is applied. A rule of thumb for locating a fastener hole is that the hole centreline should be at least 1½ times its diameter from the edge of the material. For example, the centreline of a ½ inch (12 mm) hole, should be located at least ¾ inches (18 mm) away from the edge of a plate. Because FRP is unconsolidated at the edges, this spacing value should be doubled.

When the operational load puts the fastener in tension, the problems of corrosion and nut loosening, as described previously, are still potential faults. In the case of screws, there is also a great chance that a screw, especially a wood screw, will pull out under tension. Another concern with fasteners loaded in tension is the effect they have on the relatively thin hull or deck material. When an item such as a chain plate is attached to the deck and is pulled in tension, the forces can damage the deck material. Backing plates or washers transfer the loading over a broader area and mitigate the effect of concentrated tensile or compressive loads.

All heavily loaded hardware should have a backing plate at least three inches (75 mm) in diameter. A rule of thumb for steel backing plate dimensions is that the plate diameter should be at least three times the bolt diameter and its thickness should be one-fourth the bolt diameter. Nuts should be torqued to verify their tightness and integrity. This note applies to all threaded fasteners. Tightening randomly selected nuts and screws is a good technique to verify their tightness and may reveal the weakening effects of crevice corrosion and pitting.

Check for damaged gaskets or sealants, stains indicating water leakage or actual observed leakage. Water leakage around mounted hardware will permit water to leak into the core or interlaminar cracks. To counter the problems that leaking deck components can cause to a core, some boatbuilders wisely replace the core under-deck hardware with solid FRP laminate.

Inspect for mismatched hardware, giving special attention to how aluminium and brass are used. Also inspect for frozen mechanisms such as winches and cleats, especially items that are infrequently operated. Corroded aluminium linkages are hard to detect visually so they must be operated to check their condition.

6.

Pull hard on the grab rails; if they are going to fail they should do so during the survey. Look for cracks propagating from the screw-down holes. Check the fasteners for tightness. See also the discussion on wood rot in note number 1.

7.

Toe-rails must be securely attached to the deck and should be at least 1½ inches (38 mm) high. Toe-rails can contain a great mass of

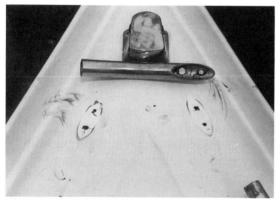

Example of very poor railing design. First, the railing was screwed into the deck. FRP will not hold a thread reliably and FRP mounted hardware should always be through-bolted. Note that cracks are radiating from all the holes. Second, no sealing plate is provided for the railing. Leaks through deck-mounted hardware is the leading cause of core saturation. Finally, the railing is simply thin-wall, chrome-plated tubing. This is very weak and on top of this, the countersinking for the screws is made simply by rolling the edge of the hole in the tubing. Note that one of the screws pulled through the railing (the right-hand hole still has its "countersink" whereas the larger left-hand hole had its "countersinking" ripped out).

water; therefore, the rail must contain plenty of scuppers.

8.

Push against the stanchions and lifelines with your foot. The stanchions should not deflect and the lifelines should hold up under a mild kick. Inspect the terminals of the lifelines and look for frayed wires or corrosion. Inspect the deck at the base of the stanchions. Large cracks radiating from this area mean that the stanchion has been overloaded – probably during docking. For offshore work, stanchions and pulpits made from pipe should be at least one inch (25 mm) in diameter and 28 inches (71 cm) high. Stanchions must be through-bolted. Check the nuts for tightness as described in note number 5.

9.

Inspect the entire drainage system. Look for leaking or damaged scuppers, flanges and hoses. Check that all hoses are double clamped and hose clamps are snug. Remember that if there is any leakage, carefully inspect the route water would travel to the bilge, as any areas where the water can collect will be a common location for corrosion, rot and damage caused by freezing water.

10.

The hatches and windows should be inspected for operation and watertightness. Look for water damage or other signs of leakage around the frames. Carefully inspect the hinges and latches – their security is critical in heavy weather. Test the watertightness of hatches and windows by spraying them with water. The American Boat and Yacht Council's specification for watertightness requires no leakage after deluging the boat with water from 10 ft (3 m) away at 15 psi (103 Pa) from a one inch (25 mm) hose for five minutes. The best technique for spraying the boat is to start at the low point in the deck and move upwards. Water will flow along all sorts of crevices until it shows itself at a low point. Therefore, by starting at the lowest deck point, the source is easier to locate. Do not trust your eyes when looking for leaks; instead feel for moisture with your fingers.

More heroic techniques for finding leaks are to seal off the boat and pressurise it with air or to seal off the boat and use an industrial smoke bomb. In the first technique, the boat can be sealed as well as possible by closing all hatches, seacocks, etc. and sealing with plastic and duct tape any vents, mast steps, companionways and the like that cannot be otherwise sealed. The discharge of a vacuum cleaner is then piped into the boat. Spraying soapy water on the hull-to-deck connection, deck hardware and cracks in the hull and deck can reveal leaks. The water will readily bubble where air is leaking. The more vigorous the bubbling, the larger the leak. Industrial smoke bombs, such as five-minute white smoke bombs, can be used on large vessels. Smoke will appear from cracks. It is important to have chalk or marking paint on hand to mark all the leaking locations during the smoking process. Be aware that smoke may cause some cosmetic damage.

11.

Well-made FRP is very strong but its weak link is in bonding sections together. Inspect the bulkheads or frames, especially where they are bonded to the hull and deck. Bulkheads are part of the boat's structure and are critical inspection points. Bulkhead-to-hull and bulkhead-to-deck connections are a common problem due to the large degree of flexing at this joint and the stress concentration caused at this junction. Look for separation of the bulkhead bonds. Push against the bulkheads while watching the bond – there should be no separation. Run an awl handle along this seam and feel for any movement. Poor bonding will be indicated by evidence of water staining, cracking or dust caused by abrasion between the two moving surfaces. Inspect the bulkhead itself for cracks, soft spots or any other indication of water damage. Another indicator of bulkhead problems is poorly fitting doors. If the doors contained within the bulkhead jam when closed or in anyway do not seem to be centred in the door jamb, this may indicate that the bulkhead has shifted causing misalignment of the door jamb and door.

12.

The proper operation of the bilge pumps, flow switches and related appurtenances are critical for the safe operation of a boat. This system is the only salvation for a vessel that has experienced a hull rupture. This equipment resides in the dirtiest, wettest and most neglected part of the boat and is therefore a very common problem. Check that all the bilge pumps have been identified. Planing boats may provide a forward bilge pump to work when the boat is off plane. Operate all electric and hand bilge pumps. The bilge pump discharge must be above waterline and preferably through the transom to avoid back-pressure by wave action.

Centrifugal pumps operate by spinning an impeller which accelerates and 'throws' the water out of the discharge. They have large capacities for their size but compared to diaphragm pumps are more sensitive to foreign material; their flow is highly dependent on inlet and discharge restriction. In addition to large flow capacities, centrifugal pumps are quiet and electrically efficient. When pumping clean water, they are more durable than other pumps because they have no wearing components and the only contacting surfaces are the shaft bearings.

Diaphragm pumps work by moving a sealed membrane back and forth that alternately draws water into the pump inlet and discharges it at a higher pressure through the outlet. Diaphragm pumps do not need to be primed before operation; they can pass small solids without damage and are generally easy to maintain and repair. It is for these reasons that they have become popular for bilge pumps. Other pumps may be encountered in bilges and *The Pump Design and Application Guide* explains centrifugal and diaphragm pumps in greater detail.

One of the most common problems with bilge pumping systems is not the pump itself but the float switch or other device that activates it. This switch must be checked thoroughly. First, operate it by hand and feel for adverse resistance to movement. Inspect it for damage or corrosion, weak mounting, poor wiring and other defects. The electrical resistance should also be measured. It must be infinite ohms when open and less than one ohm when closed. Once again, it is important to stress that the malfunction of this switch is an all too common problem and it should be inspected monthly as part of the vessel's maintenance programme. See note number 22 for more discussion of resistance measurements.

Each time a pump or motor starts, a large torque is produced. This torque stresses the pump mounts. Because of the frequent, short duration operation of the bilge pump, these mounts are often worn or cracked due to fatigue. Moreover, debris in the bilge can strike the pump system and cause damage in heavy weather.

The bilge pump system should be part of the vessel's preventative maintenance programme. That is, wearing components, or even the entire pump or switch, are replaced at prescribed time intervals rather than upon failure.

13.

Hydraulic systems should be checked for play that indicate air infiltration and any signs of fluid leakage. Hoses should be inspected for heat damage or cracking. Hoses should be supported every 2 ft (60 cm).

14.

The four common steering systems are cable, rod, geared, hydraulic and tiller. Tiller steering is a direct mechanical linkage and only needs to be inspected wherever parts can encounter wear. Hydraulic and geared systems are virtually maintenance free.

Cable systems require routine maintenance. There are a variety of cable systems available; all of them work through sheaves to transfer the rotation of the wheel to the rudder through a quadrant. Because wire cables are usually poorly lubricated, the wires in the cable wear against each other. Inspect random areas of the cable and look for wear of the individual wires and for pitting corrosion. The wire wear will be greatly accelerated if the cables are twisted.

Check sheaves for correct alignment and operation. The alignment is critical for durable operation. The cables must enter and exit the sheave on the same plane and the sheave bushing must be perpendicular to the cables. Ensure that the cable cannot ride out of the sheave and jam in the support bracket. Look for metal dust around the sheaves or quadrant. Metal dust indicates heavy wearing of a bushing or of the sheave or quadrant itself. The sheave mounts need to be inspected as described in note number 5. The mounts are usually loaded in tension and therefore should be through-bolted.

Cable stresses are inversely proportional to sheave size. Therefore, large sheaves produce lower cable stresses than small sheaves. The sheave should be at least 16 times the cable diameter. If the groove is abnormally worn, the sheave should be replaced because the action of the irregularly shaped groove will quickly wear the cable.

Chain and rod linkage systems require less maintenance than cable systems but still need to be inspected. Sprockets and chains need special attention as they are usually poorly maintained and the sprockets can wear surprisingly fast. Rod forks and connecting pins need to be carefully surveyed.

Geared systems usually do not require maintenance apart from the occasional application of sticky gear lubrication. Corrosion due to inactivity is probably the biggest problem with these systems. The commonly neglected emergency tiller must also be inspected.

See note number 17 for discussion on rudders.

15.

Inspect the propeller for damage and clearance. Propellers are carefully designed to operate efficiently based on hull type, displacement, power and operating speed. Unfortunately, these finely crafted products are often abused: they run aground, cut weeds and are abraded by sand. A common form of propeller damage is cavitation wear. Cavitation, which is the formation and implosion of bubbles on the propeller blade, can rapidly damage a propeller. Cavitation damage will usually show up on the outside edges of the blades first. Bronze propellers on stainless steel shafts are also susceptible to galvanic corrosion.

Propeller performance can be affected by small, non-visible distortions. These distortions usually manifest themselves as excessive hull vibration. However, the most important inspection for the surveyor is the hub-to-blade connection as this could cause the loss of propulsion and expose the vessel's crew to the subsequent dangers. Propellers should be gently sounded with a metal hammer, with special attention given to the area where the blades meet the hub. Listen for any flatness in sound and observe whether the sounding action flakes off any scale. The hub connection is also a good candidate for die penetrant examination. Most propellers can be repaired if they are damaged and these repairs will normally pay for themselves in decreased fuel consumption and higher top speeds.

Check the rotation of the propeller. On twin-screw boats, the propellers rotate in opposite directions. Usually the starboard propeller has a right hand rotation and the port propeller a left hand rotation. Right hand rotation is a clockwise rotation when viewed from behind the boat and left hand rotation is a counter-clockwise rotation. Most single screw boats use a right-handed propeller.

16.

Inspect the propeller shafts for any type of corrosion or bending. Pay special attention to the shaft where it exits the stuffing box, and on both sides of the strut. The shaft should be supported at least every 8 feet (2.4 m). Push the propeller shaft in all directions and feel for any play that indicates bearing wear.

Obstacles in front of a propeller will greatly diminish its performance. If a shaft collar anode is attached, ensure that it is as far forward on the shaft as possible. The anode may interfere with the smooth flow to the propeller intake. The angle that the propeller shaft makes with the waterline should be as low as possible, generally, never more than 15 degrees.

17.

Rudders can experience tremendous stresses in following seas and during manoeuvring. FRP rudders are frequently constructed from combining two half-shells. Parts made in this manner may split along the seam. Inspect the centreline of the rudder with care to look for evidence of splitting. Rudder strap screws and other mounting hardware should be inspected carefully as the heads are often sheared off.

Check the rudder for freedom of motion and condition. With the steering locked, push the rudder in all directions, including up. The amount of play will be dependent on the rudder support system and steering controls but should not be excessive.

The rule of thumb for the sizing rudder

blade on motorboats is based on a percentage of the product of the LWL and the draught. For boats of 20–35 ft (6–10 m) in length, the total rudder blade area should be five per cent of the product of LWL and draught. For boats of 35–50 ft. (10–15 m) the rudder size should be four per cent of the figure. For larger boats the rudder area decreases to three per cent of the figure. For example a boat of 4 ft (1.2 m) draught and 50 ft (15 m) LWL should have a total rudder area of $50 \times 4 \times 0.03$ or 6 ft^2 (0.54 m^2).

Trim tabs are popular features in planing hulls. These consist of pairs of stainless steel after-planes secured to the stern. These planes are usually hydraulically controlled from the helm. These planes need to be inspected for collision damage, bearing wear or any other anomaly.

18.

Stringers and the engine bed, along with bulk-heads and ribs, tie a boat's structure together and are critical inspection points. Inspect the stringers and engine bed for cracking, warpage or separation from the hull. Pay special attention to the end of the stringers and under the engine mounts. The sharp corners produced where wooden structural members that have been covered by fibreglass meet the hull are a source of stress concentration and need to be inspected as described in note number 11. Rot commonly starts where the stringers or frame attaches to the planking on wooden boats.

19.

It is not possible to cover all the installation recommendations for mechanical and electrical systems. However, several regulatory bodies and advisory councils have specific installation recommendations and requirements. See Appendices 1&2.

20.

Engine installations along with trans-missions, shafts and propellers are usually dictated by the engine manufacturers. Installation guidelines are specific to the vessel's intended use and whether the engine is diesel or petrol-fired.

Some sources of common engine and propulsion systems problems can be addressed by these highlights:

• If the engine air intake is not ducted outside, intake air should be vented so that it is no more than 30°F (16°C) higher than the ambient air. For air inlet temperatures above 100°F (38°C), the engine horsepower decreases 1 per cent for every 10°F (5.5°C) increase in the temperature of air inlet.

• The exhaust manifold should not directly support the engine exhaust system. As the exhaust system heats up and expands, the manifold would bear all the induced stress if it was rigidly supporting the exhaust. If the exhaust piping rises vertically from the manifold, riser clamps or some other means to support the exhaust is required.

• Exhaust gases must be discharged far away from intake vents so that they do not affect the air cleaner or get drawn onboard– on wet exhausts, this is usually not a problem. With dry exhaust systems, the exhaust must be sufficiently high and abaft to keep the exhaust clear of the boat.

• On a wet exhaust system, ensure that the exhaust riser is not leaking or weakened by corrosion.

• The rate of galvanic corrosion increases with elevated temperature. Carefully inspect engine exhaust and coolant systems. Brass fittings are sometimes used in the flexible lines of the coolant system and these can galvanically corrode steel and other anodic metals.

• All external engine connections (e.g. fuel, coolant, air and exhaust) should have a flexible connection between the engine and the hull.

Give special attention to the flexible connections in the exhaust system. Look for damage due to thermal expansion or degradation.

• Adequate oil pressure must be maintained under all conditions. Good oil pressure is required for reliable engine performance – not to mention engine durability. The surveyor should advise the owner to monitor the oil pressure when the oil level is low and the boat is at maximum trim.

• Black exhaust smoke is caused by incomplete combustion. Common causes are:

1. Intake air restriction.
2. Exhaust restriction.
3. Poor fuel quality.

• White exhaust smoke indicates unburned fuel. This is usually due to incomplete combustion resulting from low engine cylinder temperatures. Common causes include:

1. Cold ambient air.
2. Water in fuel.
3. Faulty thermostat.
4. Incorrect engine timing.
5. Fuel pump surging.
6. Fuel injector problems.

• Vibration can consist of linear and torsional movements. Linear vibration is the common movement that we can see. Torsional vibration is the twisting of an object back and forth. This sort of vibration cannot be seen but can be heard as gear chattering and can result in clutch and gear damage. Engine vibration can be caused by:

1. Loose mounting bolts.
2. Damaged vibration damper.
3. Misfiring engine.
4. High oil level.
5. Flexible engine-bed.
6. Power take-off (PTO) or drive shaft misalignment.

• Thumping or stern rumble can be caused by:

1. Cavitation caused by the propeller passing too close to the hull.
2. Strut located too close to the front of the propeller.

If these are the source of noise, it will have a frequency three times the shaft speed with a three-bladed propeller, and four times the shaft speed with a four-bladed propeller.

Other thumping sounds can be produced by torsional vibrations that may result from:

1. Unbalanced propeller.
2. Bent or misaligned propeller shaft.
3. Improperly designed propulsion system.

21.

The experienced ear and diagnostic devices of a professional mechanic are indispensable in assessing an engine's condition. The engine rebuild schedule is determined by the manufacturer but is normally every 1,500 hours. Oil samples can be sent to a testing laboratory for evaluation. However, this method of engine monitoring is most often used by organisations with many engines such as bus and truck fleets. The technique is better used to look at trends rather than the condition of the engine at any particular time.

22.

Trace the entire fuel system. The critical points to examine are the fuel lines, fuel tank and electrical grounding. The fuel fill pipe must be tightly fastened to the fill plate. All hoses, clamps and pipes routed from the fill pipe to the fuel tank should be given special attention. Fuel must not be permitted to gravity flow to the engine through the supply line or injector return lines when the engine is shut off.

A small spraying leak in a pressurised fuel line is more dangerous than a complete severing of the line. The spraying fuel is more likely to create an explosive air-to-fuel mixture than a puddle of fuel. Moreover, spraying fuel is more likely to contact an ignition source. For this reason, ensure that all fuel hoses meet statutory requirements. Check that the hoses are not kinked and will not abrade against something during vessel operation.

The fuel system must be grounded to avoid the development of an electrical charge due to the flowing of the fuel (which has literally blown up ships). Measure the electrical resistance between any point on the fuel system and the electrical ground. This can be done by clipping one end of an ohmmeter to the electrical bonding strap, preferably near the battery, and touching the other end to the tank, filler plate and other fuel system components. The resistance measurement should be less than a few ohms. The bonding must also be measured from the furthest ends to the battery. Any resistance in the ground bonding must be investigated. A resistance measurement of above say, 20 ohms, may include the resistance of a coil (such as in a solenoid valve or motor). When measuring resistance with an ohmmeter or continuity probe, a DC signal is sent through the line. With a DC signal, coils appear as a relatively low resistance. However, coils are very 'resistive' (AC resistance is referred to as *reactance*) at AC frequencies. What this means is that a solenoid coil or motor could be connected in the grounding system and it would appear to have a very low resistance, yet these coils would incapacitate the grounding system when the AC is operating. (See 'Note' number 29 for further information on grounding).

The fuel tank must be securely mounted and not move in any direction at the mounting points. The tank must adequately vent air and prevent the entrance of dirt or water. All lines must be drawn from the top of the tank, including the fuel suction line. The suction line should have an anti-siphon hole to prevent fuel from flowing to the engine or generator after it is shut down.

Tanks are commonly made from monel or aluminium. Galvanised steel is not a good choice because the zinc plating can flake off (especially with diesel fuel) and plug the fuel filters. The welds are the usual source of leakage problems on fuel tanks. Fuel tanks that are integral to the hull are subject to all the loads of the hull. A special suspicion must be kept for these tanks. High-speed boats should have the fuel tank attached through rubber shock mounts and adjustable straps.

23.

Anchors, shackles, chains and rode need to be inspected carefully for cracks or deformation. Pay special attention to the shackles, rode and eyes and liberally use die penetrant.

Lines need to be inspected for any signs of degradation or weak points. Sharp bends and knots decrease the line strength by as much as 50 per cent. Slippage or surging on a capstan or winch can cause overheating of a line around these devices. Overheating will weaken the line. Synthetic ropes can lose 50 per cent of their strength when exposed to temperatures above 140°F (60°C). Lines should be stored in a cool, dry and well-ventilated location that is out of direct sunlight. Natural fibre cordage must be carefully stored as it will mildew quickly if stored in a damp location

24.

The potable water system may simply consist of a water tank and hand-operated diaphragm pumps at the faucets. Manual pumping draws water into the pump and is discharged from the faucet. More elaborate water systems usually consist of several storage tanks, an accumulator tank, pump, pressure switch, inlet and outlet connectors. Water is pumped from the water tank into an accumulator tank. As the water fills the accumulator tank it compresses the enclosed air bladder. The accumulator tank is pumped up until the pressure switch stops the pump. The compressed air maintains a constant pressure on the water and eliminates water pressure pulsation and rapid on/off pump cycling. This not only extends the water pump life but also permits smooth water flow to all fixtures.

The inlet deck connection allows the water tanks to be filled. Outlet connections are usually provided to allow pressurised dock-side water to be used directly in the boat's system. A pressure regulator with a backflow preventer should be used when external water can directly pressurise the boat's system to prevent overpressuring of the boat's system.

Operate the faucets and listen for the sound of the water pump. It should sound very smooth. Inspect the piping for leaks. Steel or copper pipes can develop pinhole leaks due to corrosion. Any kinks in either copper or vinyl tubing need to be pointed out, as they are not only flow restrictions, but also likely sources of failure.

Although vinyl tubing seems flexible and easy to handle, at low temperatures it gets rigid and brittle. Vinyl's thermal expansion coefficient is five to six times that of steel; therefore, if a boat is exposed to freezing conditions, the combination of brittleness and thermal contraction can easily break the tubing. If the tubing is fitted to a PVC or nylon-barbed fitting, the fitting itself is likely to break at low temperatures. Brass or stainless steel barbed fittings are preferred, especially for elbows, because they can accept the tightening of band clamps better than PVC and nylon. Moreover, brass or stainless steel threaded adapters have much stronger threads and are therefore less likely to be damaged during installation.

The sanitation system will consist of the head, holding tank, waste diverter Y-valve and associated plumbing. Most marine heads work by pumping in seawater and discharging the effluent into a holding tank or overboard with a macerator pump. The macerator pump is a pump with a cutting blade that reduces the size of the effluent. Vacuum systems are also common in larger boats.

Blockage of the sanitation system is a messy but common problem. This often occurs at the diverter valve. Check the operation of the system by pumping water into the head and checking that it can be pumped overboard. Carefully inspect the mounting base of the head to ensure its integrity.

25.

It will be a happy day when open flames are eliminated from boats, until then these systems must be used with great care and inspected thoughtfully. Witnessing smoke pour out of the companionway when hundreds of miles at sea gives a good appreciation of the need for convenient fire extinguishers and cooking safety. Check the stove for a uniform flame. A sputtering flame as well as a flame with dark or yellow-orange streaks indicates poor combustion or air in the fuel. Some stoves have a temperature sensor that automatically turns the gas off in the absence of a flame. This interface can be checked by blowing out the flame when it is set very low and listening for the gas to stop flowing. If it does not shut off soon after the flame is blown out, turn the gas off and vent the area.

26.

Leakage of fuel can be detected by listening and smelling. With propane or CNG (compressed natural gas), use a soapy water solution to spray on connections and fittings. If there is leakage, the solution will readily bubble. No leakage whatsoever is acceptable. If the tank is equipped with a pressure gauge, leaks can be detected by measuring any pressure drop in the tank with the entire system pressurised. To do this, open the tank valve and electrical solenoid and pressurise the system for at least 15 minutes. A fuel leak exists if the tank pressure drops during this time (The U.S. *National Fuel Gas Code* requires that home fuel gas systems exhibit no leakage while pressurised at 1½ times the operation pressure for at least ten minutes.) Use soapy water to locate the leak.

Propane is heavier than air and therefore is very dangerous if it enters the boat. Inside the boat it will settle in the bilge and can, when ignited by some source, either burn or explode depending on the ratio of gas to air. Both are disastrous. It is imperative that the propane tank be stored in a locker that is completely separate from the rest of the vessel. The storage locker must also be bottom vented outside so that an explosive mixture cannot develop within it. CNG is lighter than air and, with adequate ventilation, will not develop an explosive mixture in the bilge.

27.

Freezers, refrigerators and air conditioners are all considered to be refrigeration equipment. They typically work by compressing a refrigerant gas (commonly a mixture of Freon grades) into a liquid then passing it through an evaporator that absorbs surrounding heat by boiling the liquid into a gas. The gas is recompressed by a compressor pump, and under the pressure produced by the pump, recondenses into a liquid in the condenser. The cooling temperatures are controlled by the amount of fluid that passes through the system and is regulated by an expansion valve. This cycle repeats continuously until the desired temperature is achieved.

The external features that make a refrigeration cycle work are the heat exchanger (cooling coils) and fans. These can be visually inspected and the condition of the heat exchanger fins should be noted. Freon leaks will quickly reduce the ability of the system to cool and eventually make the system completely ineffectual. Therefore, leaks are simply checked by performance. If power is available, check that the equipment cools down, using a thermometer, a finger or a glass of water. Listen for unusual noises. Check the

charge status of the system by either observing an indicator light or pressure gauge. The other external features on freezers and refrigerators are the condensate drains or sump pumps. Confirm that the condensate drains are not plugged and that any sump pumps operate correctly.

Freon released to the atmosphere depletes the ozone layer; therefore, Freon compositions are changing. In some cases, different Freon compositions can be used in a refrigeration system by simply changing the expansion valve. This is not always the case. Recharging and servicing of a refrigeration system must be done by a qualified technician.

28.

All fabrics should be inspected for tears, scuffs, wear, adrift threads, mildew and fading. Slip an awl or pin under some of the threads, they should not pull out or break under moderate pressure. This probing technique is the same one used to evaluate most sewn material such as safety harnesses and PFDs.

Check the condition and operation of snaps and zippers. Inspect plastic windows for fogging and cracking.

29.

A boat's DC electrical system usually consists of an alternator, regulator, batteries, battery switch, circuit breakers or fuses, voltmeter, ammeter and wiring. The boat may also have a battery isolator and inverter. The shore power system will consist of circuit breakers or fuses, battery charger and wiring. Electrical systems can be diagnosed by tracing voltages. The most common problems usually involve grounding and terminal connections.

The battery switch should be inspected for dirty or arc damaged contacts. The battery terminals, battery and engine grounds should be checked to ensure they are clean and securely fastened. The battery mounting should also be inspected to confirm that it rigidly holds the batteries in position at all trims and even during a capsize – leaking battery acid will make a bad situation worse.

Electrical wiring should be inspected as much as practical. Solid wire fatigues easier than does stranded wire and should be given special attention. Confirm the security of as many terminal connections as practical by tugging gently on the them. The wiring harnesses should be secured every six inches (15 cm). Pay special attention to the bilge pump wiring because it gets the most abuse.

Good grounding is required for protecting the fuel system (see 'Note', number 22), lightning protection, radio and antenna performance. Moreover, good grounding will usually eliminate stray current corrosion. All electrical items need to be grounded, this includes: fuel tanks and other fuel components, generators, engines, alternator frames, electrical control panels, electrical conduits, battery trays, bilge pumps, all large electrical accessories and for non-metallic hulls, ground plates. Sometimes the propeller shaft must be grounded by contacting brushes when the rotating shaft produces radio frequency interference. The mast or highest metallic object should also be grounded to provide some lightning protection. The grounding, or bonding, of electrical items is usually accomplished by a heavy copper wire, strap or pipe. In metal hulls, the ground can be run directly from the equipment to the hull. Maintaining all equipment at the same ground potential will eliminate stray current corrosion except when it is produced by crossed grounds or stray AC electrical voltages such as can occur in marinas. Crossed grounds occur when one piece of DC equipment has its negative pole attached to the electrical ground while another piece is grounded to the positive pole. DC equipment should always be grounded to the same polarity (usually the negative terminal is grounded). The AC system must be entirely separate from the DC system. The AC neutral must never be attached to the

grounding system. However, AC equipment should have their frames or a grounding wire attached to ground

30.
The navigation equipment should be inventoried. It should not be operated unless requested by the owner. Each piece of equipment such as GPS, LORAN, RDF, radar and autopilots should be tested and operated in accordance with their accompanying operating manuals. Common equipment such as depth sounders, logs, wind speed and direction indicators can be operated to confirm their function.

31.
Connecting a dummy load to the transceiver's antenna connector can check the transmitting performance of transceivers such as Marine VHF, Marine SSB, Amateur and CB (a transmitter may not be operated without the required licence). A dummy load is a large resistor that presents an ideal antenna load to the transmitter. With the dummy load attached to the transmitter the transmitter can be tested without radiating a strong signal. In addition to checking modulation, the maximum possible power of the transmitter can be observed. An SWR (Standing Wave Ratio) meter can be used to determine how well the antenna matches the transmitter. SWR is dependent on the operating frequency and should ideally be 1:1. The ability of a transmitter to accept a higher SWR is dependent on the transmitter design. An SWR of less than 2:1 on the desired operating frequencies is usually acceptable. An SWR of 2:1 means that 10 per cent of the transmitted power is reflected back to the transmitter and wasted rather than radiating from the antenna. Most modern transmitters will shut themselves off automatically if the SWR gets over 3:1 (25 per cent reflected power).

Antenna performance in the shortwave bands as are used for Marine SSB is strongly affected by the quality of the radio frequency ground. Consequently, antenna performance will be degraded on a hauled boat.

32.

Confirming the presence and operation of safety equipment is one of the most important roles of the surveyor. Probably the most common cause for classing societies to condemn vessels is inoperative safety equipment. Required safety equipment is usually dictated by the force of law. Applicable statutes must be referenced. (See Appendix 1) The following items are typical of required safety items for boats venturing offshore. Once again, it is important to refer to applicable national or classing statutes pertaining to the size and application of the boat being surveyed.

- Personal and throwable floatation devices
  (record: quantity, types, locations)

- Visual distress signals
  (record: quantity, types, locations, expiration dates)

- Portable and automatic fire extinguishers
  (record: quantity, types, locations and recharge dates)

- Fuel ventilation

- Backfire flame control (spark arrester)

- Sound-producing devices (record types)

- Bilge pumps
  (confirm operation, soundness of installation; record: quantity, types, capacity)

- MOB (man overboard) pole

- Radar reflector

- First aid kit

- EPIRB (Emergency Position Indicating Radio Beacon)

(record: quantity, types, locations, expiration dates)

- Liferaft
  (Check liferaft for valid inspection certificate. Only canister types may be mounted on deck. Valise types must be mounted in a watertight compartment.)

Personal safety gear such as PFDs, harnesses, survival suits, strobe lights and whistles should not be part of the survey. These are very portable items and their assessment is beyond the scope of the surveyor's expertise.

33.

Some safety features such as toe-rails, stanchions and lifelines have been discussed elsewhere. Other safety issues for a deck crew are pinch points, sharp edges, trip ups, and loose objects. These threats must be thoroughly evaluated. Injuries at sea are especially serious. This is not only due to the risk to the injured party but, to a much lesser extent, the impact it will have on the rest of the crew. Short-crewed boats are common and if a crew member has a badly cut hand, he cannot do his tasks. Cuts heal slowly at sea because of the reluctance to properly nurse the injuries when there is work to do. The continual chaffing of the wound because of the attempt to perform normal duties, along with immersion of the wound in salt water will make the crew member miserable.

Start a safety inspection by looking in the most unused perspective – up. Check for free swinging hoists, spars, gates, doors and similar items that could swing and hit someone. Pinch points and sharp edges are more obvious. Pinch points are common in boats. They exist wherever two items can close down on a hand, foot or limb. Some are obvious to the crew and are handled with care, such as where the windlass and anchor chains meet. Some are less clear. For example, closing a hatch without a handle or hand relief could easily hurt someone when it is closed in a churning sea. Or when the hatch is opened it drops with great force onto the deck and possibly onto someone's foot. Because 'one hand is for the ship', all tasks have to be accomplished by a one-handed, tired crewman on a tossing deck. Grab rails should be used liberally above and below deck.

There is no excuse for sharp edges on a boat. This includes all deck, below deck and superstructure features. Trim moulding will round out joints; caps can be snapped onto protruding screws and bolts. Metal objects must have rounded edges. Rigging must have no loose wires. When all else fails, sharp edges can be taped or covered by a polyurethane or silicone adhesive to reduce the hazard they present to the crew.

The helmsman, regardless of whether he is the first mate or an ambitious passenger, is responsible for three things: obstacles, draught and course. Whoever is holding the wheel is responsible for ensuring the boat will not run into anything (including the ground) and holding the prescribed course. When the skipper has his face buried in charts or is jammed into the engine room, he cannot be expected to watch for all these things. Consequently, these three tasks must be easily accomplished. This means there should be excellent visibility from the helm, a conveniently-located depth sounder and compass. There are often many blind spots for the helmsman, the positioning of equipment in front of the bridge must be considered with respect to visibility. Cameras and lookouts can offset some blind spots.

The following items must be accessible from the helm: engine controls, fire extinguisher, horn, throwable PFD, man overboard pole, binoculars and an emergency tiller on sailboats. Engine alarms or gauges must also be available at the helm. Safety harnesses, PFDs and other safety items must also be conveniently located. Radar is also required near the helm when used. Movable electronic charts that interface with GPS and radar can add enormous convenience and safety to the helm.

The features that make a boat easy to handle are not strictly a concern for the surveyor. However, it is very difficult to remain neutral about items that will make the crew's life miserable. To keep the crew happy, they must be safe, warm, dry, rested and well fed. The latter two concerns are the domain of good management. Keeping the crew warm and dry can be accomplished by good foul weather gear; however, it is to everyone's advantage when this can be assisted by the boat design. In my own experience, when sailing in cold, iceberg-laden waters, I was reluctant to turn my head to look for bergs because every time I did, the wind would blow down my hood and drive away the hard-earned body warmth. It is human nature to try to take short cuts whenever possible. Therefore, anticipate that the wheel will be held with the helmsman's foot while tying fenders to the lifelines. Where are the engine controls? Will they be moved during this process? In cold weather climates, a pilot house is invaluable. High cockpit coamings and a dodger will help keep the crew dry. A bimini will keep the tropical sun at bay. Scuppers are required for safety in that they rapidly remove the huge mass of water that can fill decks and cockpits. They must be logically placed and designed to ensure that water will drain completely at all hull angles.

The location of frequently used items must be logical and of suitable quality. Sailors spend almost as much time interfacing with the winches as with the helm. Sir Francis Chichester expended several paragraphs in his book *Gipsy Moth Circles the World* deriding his faulty winches. Cam cleats, stoppers, deck space between the cabin and the lifelines, and hatch features are all small things that can be enormously frustrating for the blue water sailor.

34.

Keel integrity is critical to the safety of a boat. Unfortunately, it is one of the most difficult parts of a craft to assess. Removal or X-raying of the keel bolts and the manufacturer's recommendations are the best approach to keel diagnosis. However, the following two paragraphs outline inspections that can also provide some insights into the keel connection.

On an externally ballasted keel there should be no sign of movement between the hull and keel. This will show up as cracked paint, water or oil stains. It is important to note that the appearance of the bolt ends and nuts is no indication of the condition of the entire bolt. If there is any question about the integrity of the keel connection, recommend the replacement of the keel bolts.

For poured-in-place ballast, the keel should be sounded to detect separation from the ballast. In addition, the keel sump should be inspected to confirm that it is sealed. Sealing the keel is important in preventing damage to the keel FRP from the expansive force of freezing water.

35.

Inspect the base of the mast for corrosion. Keel-stepped masts are most likely to show corrosion because they are often immersed in water. Any movement of the bottom of the mast will cause rapid wear.

36.

The wires that make up the shroud and stays should lie properly in the cable. They should not be broken, kinked, adrift or corroded. Wires that run nearly straight in the cable suggest that it has been overstressed. Inspect swage connections with great care, they are very thin and handle high loads. The terminals should be checked with a dye penetrant. They should be sealed with silicone to prevent salt or moisture from entering and producing crevice corrosion. Standing rigging more than ten years old should be given special consideration and the manufacturer's recommendations for inspection or replacement must always be followed.

If the stays and shrouds seem over-tight, inspect the mast step carefully to find any damage produced by this strong downward pull on the mast.

Galvanic corrosion may occur at the ends of spreaders due to contact with the stainless steel shrouds.

37.

The sail-cloth and reinforcements should be checked for tears, chaffing, adrift threads and discolouration. Slip an awl or pin under some of the threads – they should not pull out or break under moderate pressure.

Most sails are made from Dacron and will be weakened by ultraviolet light. A more thorough inspection of the sail can be done at a sail loft but it should be noted that deformation of the sail cannot be detected unless the sail is hoisted and filled.

Design and Application Guides

Hull Design and Application Guide

Hulls do more than carry the weight of cargo, machinery and personnel – they define the purpose of the craft. In the endeavour to efficiently separate and move us on the water, hulls have been refined to the point of truly beautiful structures. Looking at a hauled vessel, the surveyor should have a good understanding of hull performance based on proportions. Normal sea trials will not expose the vessel to all the forces of nature and a hull shape will give some flavour of the vessel's unique characteristics.

Hull designs were originally developed by instinct and experience. However, mature designs quickly incorporated the local religious beliefs, social values, superstitions and aesthetic values. Ceremonies such as adding the milk from a mother nursing her first child to the boat's caulking are still performed today. They reflect the trust seaman must have in their vessels, especially when a liferaft, EPIRB and the like are not part of the inventory.

The direct approach to hull design is to optimise the shape to provide 1) stability 2) speed and 3) load-carrying ability. The waters plied mitigate the relative importance of these factors. In calm water, less stability is required of the hull than for an ocean-going vessel. In fast rivers, great speed is required to advance against the current and maintain steerage downstream.

Great load-carrying ability is one of the most essential requirements for any vessel. It dictates the length, beam and draught. The ability to efficiently carry huge amounts of cargo is what maintains shipping into the twenty-first century. In shipbuilding there is a painful design movement between speed and efficiency, efficiency generally meaning good fuel efficiency; however, it also means low operating costs (small crew, fast cargo handling and no tug assistance). Cargo transportation is now done on large, slow and efficient ships – most merchant ships are designed to travel at less than 20 knots.

High-speed, ocean passenger travel is now an anachronism. The great, high-speed passenger ships like the *Mauretania*, *United States* and *Queen Mary* are gone. People travel by cruise ship to enjoy the sea. If they were in any kind of hurry (or on a restrictive budget) they would fly to their destination. High speed also means much higher fuel costs.

Shipping hulls have been greatly affected by cargo requirements and labour costs. Labour costs increased tenfold between 1950 and 1970 bringing about more efficient and easier to load ships. For example in the early 1960s open hatch ships came into prominence. These ships have decks with huge hatches, in fact there is very little permanent deck on this design – quite a structural challenge. These large openings allowed rapid loading by onboard jib cranes. At the same time hatches in the sides of hulls started appearing. This design allowed forklifts to gain easy access to the holds.

Many ships have been designed for specific applications in order to improve their overall efficiency. For example OBO (ore-bulk-oil) ships are uniquely suited to carry oil on one route and grain on the return route. The ubiquitous container ships with their stacks of standard sized (8 foot square by 20 or 40 feet long, 2.4 metre square by 6 or 12 m long) aluminium-alloy containers can quickly interface with trains and trucks to provide tremendous efficiency (although with an obvious disregard for appearance). The container ship's measure of capacity in TEUs (Twenty Foot Equivalent Unit) has become the new unit of cargo-carrying ability. Gas carriers are another specialised ship design that has the onerous task of carrying, $-260°F$ $(-162°C)$ liquefied natural gas across oceans and into crowded harbours. For shorter distances, high-speed vessels have taken the form of catamarans, hovercrafts and hydrofoils.

Workboats usually pull (or push) boats, barges or nets. These boats typically have small crews and the hulls are built around massive engines, holds and winches. One dramatic change in workboats is the rapid increase in fishing boat size. Large, stern-ramp trawlers are able to travel worldwide, dragging their nets through all the world's fishing havens.

The word 'yacht' comes from the Dutch word 'jachtschiff' meaning 'hunting ship'. Yachts are boats intended for recreation and comfort and have been part of the trappings of power since the ancient Egyptians. Their designs vary widely from sailboats and planing powerboats to slow, efficient, 'trawlers'. Catamarans are becoming increasingly popular in yacht design.

Hull Shapes

Hulls are defined by their shape. Common hull designations are *displacement*, *semi-displacement* and *planing*. Besides the general hull shape, the other features of the hull are determined by its performance and operational requirements. For example, the beam is decided by such things as stability, cargo requirement, crew comfort in beam seas, width of dry docks and slips, canal width maximums and so on. In similar fashion, the length and draught are determined. All these dimensions must provide the required buoyancy. The amount of stem and stern overhang are determined by the required reserve stability. Other design subtleties are determined by combinations of operating needs and aesthetics. Aesthetics has a very important role in yacht design although not that much more than in workboats. It is always a good design goal to make a product *look* as if it was intended to perform its function. For example, fast boats must look fast. This is often done with raked features: low freeboard, aerodynamic radar masts, etc. High alloy steels can be many times thinner than cast bronze, but massive bronze deck hardware will inspire more confidence and is sometimes thought to be an indicator of overall boat quality. It is not uncommon for an owner to specify some arcane components to be included in the boat design because the owner is convinced of their superior quality.

Displacement Hull

A displacement hull simply forces water past its bow and sides as it is propelled through the water. Very stable in heavy weather and employing uncomplicated arch-like or box sections, displacement hulls are used on most workboats, sailboats and ships. The maximum speed of a displacement hull is constrained by its length. As the hull is forced through the water, a bow wave is produced. When the speed of the vessel is such that the peak of the wave is in sync. with the trough produced at the stern – a resonance of sorts, the hull cannot go faster regardless of additional power. If the hull is driven harder, the stern squat increases and constrains the forward speed.

Displacement hulls provide a large amount of interior space relative to other hull shapes. They are relatively easy to build, stable and seaworthy. Moreover, they have excellent economy of operation, using relatively small engines and having low fuel consumption. The low fuel consumption translates to a much longer cruising range than any planing hull. This is the oldest seagoing design and is certainly the ideal hull design – if speed is not an issue. Low speed is the displacement hull's biggest disadvantage although super carriers can travel at 35 knots with the benefit of 280,000 hp driving the screws.

Semi-Displacement

Semi-displacement hulls are an important design as they are commonly used on large vessels requiring greater speed. Semi-displacement hulls typically employ straighter bottoms, wider transoms, lighter displacement and more power than displacement hulls. The flatter underbody allows the boat to rise above the bow wave. They are more sea kindly than planing hulls yet not as seaworthy as displacement hulls. Given suitable power, a semi-displacement hull can be driven nearly twice as fast as a displacement hull. With enough power, for example, a 50 ft (15 m) semi-displacement hull can travel at nearly 18 knots.

Planing

Planing hulls liberate the boat from the grasp of the water and therefore free the vessel from the effect of the powerful stern squatting phenomenon of displacement hulls. The liberation of the hull is achieved by using the forward motion of the boat to give it hydro-dynamic lift. The boat literally pulls itself out of the water and dramatically decreases the wetted hull surface. This feature is achieved by making a hull with a flat bottom and broad beam.

Older designs for planing hulls had steep deadrise, V-shaped sections that flattened quickly amidships. They employed a skeg for directional stability. Although this design was capable of obtaining high S/L ratios and subsequent speed, it produced pounding rides when working through waves. The 'deep V' hull was developed to provide a smoother ride in a planing hull. The deep V profile maintains a V-shaped, moderate deadrise through to the transom. This shape gives a smoother ride in the waves and eliminates the need for a skeg.

Planing hulls are very popular because of their speed. This is certainly an important commodity in many marine applications. Perhaps because they finish their task so quickly, they can better suffer the disadvantages they have with respect to displacement hulls. These disadvantages include higher power requirements with the accompanying increase in operating cost and decrease in range.

They have less interior space, especially after the large powerplant is accounted for. Their performance is sensitive to trim, so load location must be carefully planned. They are inefficient at low speeds and their beamy shallow hulls with hard chines give them an uncomfortable ride.

Catamarans

Catamarans have been used in India and the Pacific Islands for ages. Catamarans were used in medieval Europe as a matter of necessity when a single hull could not carry a heavy cargo. Now they are used to great advantage in both sailing yachts and powerboats. They provide a hull with light displacement and low drag. Their only limitations are the large turning radius required when steered with rudder alone and the construction difficulties.

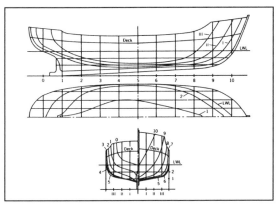

Displacement Hull

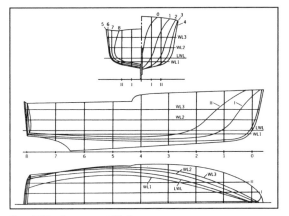

Semi-Displacement Hull

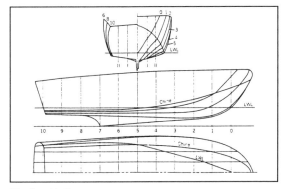

Planing Hull

Although there are a variety of catamaran designs, they usually use U-shaped hulls with a length-to-beam ratio ranging from 8:1 to 16:1. This high ratio gives them a very low pressure drag. Catamarans are typically designed with an overall beam equal to one half the LWL. They obtain their stability from a wide beam and therefore do not need ballast. Consequently, they can have a much lighter displacement than a similarly sized monohull. The high stability is especially attractive in sailboats because it eliminates the need for massive lead in the keel to lower the centre of gravity. Therefore, not only can the same sail-carrying ability be offered by a much lighter craft but they can also be more easily made unsinkable by the use of internal floatation. The problem with the catamaran's wide beam and high centre of gravity is that it cannot be made self-righting, and if it tips over, it will not right itself like a traditional, heavy displacement sailboat.

Often, a nacelle is provided between the hulls that sits just above the waterline. This acts like a third hull and offers additional reserve buoyancy although its principal role is to increase headroom. Many catamarans may have either full bridge-decks, meaning the deck is solid between the two hulls, or partial bridge-decks with a trampoline or netting across the bows. Racing-style catamarans such as the popular Hobie-Cats have no solid deck between the hulls and are referred to as open wings.

Compared to monohulls, catamarans are faster and offer a shallower draught. These are very attractive attributes. On top of these advantages, sailing catamarans do not heel significantly and have smaller sail requirements. There has been a great deal of debate about the seaworthiness of catamarans. Generally, they are not considered to be as seaworthy as monohulls principally because of their lack of self-righting ability and also because they are anything but monolithic. With complex hull connections, shallow draught and a broad deck, they do not seem to be able to handle breaking waves well. However, they do have two separate, lightweight hulls. Often these hulls are designed to be buoyant when fully flooded. Therefore, they have a high survivability factor. Catamarans are more expensive than monohulls and it is more difficult to find sufficiently wide slips in most marinas.

Other Designs

Fortunately, hull design sometimes advances radically to proffer such novel designs as hydrofoils, surface effect vehicles, and small water plane twin hulls (SWATH). These designs are far removed from the common hulls currently in service, which are virtually unchanged from antiquity.

These advanced boat designs – certainly there is more to their performance than hull shape alone – are cousins of the planing hull. These designs try, by various means, to lift the inefficient mass of hull out of the water and free it from the drag and wave making produced by driving a hull through the water.

Hydrofoils have lifting plates, called foils, mounted fore and aft. The foils are attached to the hull by struts. When a hydrofoil comes up on plane, it does it in spectacular fashion. The angle of the foils forces the entire hull out of the water leaving only the foils and their connecting struts piercing through the water. Surface-piercing foils are also used. These foils actually rise almost completely out of the water and act just like water skis. Hydrofoils do not handle waves well and are usually used on calm waters.

Watching a huge hovercraft fly across the water then drive up onto the shore is a fascinating sight. Hovercrafts have powerful fans that develop a pocket of pressurized air under the hull. A hovercraft is one category of surface effect vehicles. Hovercrafts ride on an air cushion, which eliminates the resistance associated with travel through water. When the importance of a flexible skirt around the craft was finally realised, these naval helicopters became viable craft. The skirt keeps the pressurized air from blowing out from under the hull. Propulsion is developed using aircraft-type propellers. Consequently, the craft can operate on land or sea. The propeller pitch can be changed to control speed and provide braking.

Captured air bubble or tunnel boats are surface effect craft that are a mixture of hovercraft and catamaran. Although there are a variety of specific designs, they basically work by trapping air under the boat between the catamaran hulls. The trapped air lifts the boat up and reduces its wetted surface. This action decreases the drag and consequently increases the speed. These boats are not as fast as hydrofoils but can be used in rougher water.

SWATH (small water plane twin hull) shapes are catamarans that have deeply submerged hulls. The hulls are attached to the vessel by thin supporting struts. This feature reduces drag by reducing the wave-making characteristics of the boat.

Speed-to-Length Ratio

The 'speed-to-length ratio' (or S/L ratio) is a convenient way to describe the relationship between the size of the bow wave and the length of the hull. The S/L ratio is used to categorise hull shapes and relate them to maximum hull speed.

The speed-to-length ratio is defined as follows:

$$S/L = \text{speed in knots} \div \sqrt{LWL} \text{ in feet}$$

where, L = LWL
LWL is the only issue that is of concern when looking at hulls. The length overall (LOA), with the exception of the sea kindly effects of overhangs that will be discussed later, is basically an advertising number.

The maximum hull speed is then calculated as:

$$\text{Maximum speed (knots)} = \text{speed-to-length ratio} \times \sqrt{\text{length (feet)}}$$

The speed-to-length ratio is dependent on the particularities of the hull shape. A symmetrical hull shape will produce the speed-limiting squatting phenomenon at an S/L ratio of 1.4. Therefore for a symmetrical, full-bodied displacement hull with a S/L ratio maximum of 1.4, a 50 ft (15 m) boat will have a limiting speed of: $1.4 \times \sqrt{50} = 10$ knots. A fine bow and flat stern increases the maximum S/L ratio as it becomes more of a semi-displacement hull. The flatter stern resists squatting. A broad bow and stern will decrease the S/L ratio.

Different hull shapes have different maximum S/L ratios as described below.

Typical S/L ratios	
Displacement hulls	0.80–1.4
Semi-displacement hull	1.4–2.5
Planing hull	2.5–

Drag

As described in the 'Primer on Fluid Mechanics', drag is produced by skin friction, poor streamlining and wave-making energy. As speed increases, all of these drag forms increase for most hulls. Friction drag can only be reduced by smoothing out the vessel's wetted surface. Every animal that moves quickly through earthly fluids of air and water is streamlined. Streamlining reduces pressure drag. Flat surfaces facing the flow of a fluid produce high pressure while flat surfaces at the back of an object create low pressure and strong energy-consuming eddies down-

stream. Barges typically have these flat fore and aft features and subsequently have a very low speed-to-length ratio of around 0.8. The key to efficient passage through a fluid is to produce gradual changes in direction. Not only does this reduce eddies but it also reduces the drag produced by making waves. Therefore, a boat that was intended to move slowly through the water, where squatting is not an issue, would have a very fine hull and stern section. These features would allow it to slice through water and gently replace it astern. Canoes and kayaks fit nicely into this category.

While moving water horizontally creates pressure drag, moving it vertically produces wave-making drag. This wave-making drag is also reduced by streamlining the hull.

Hull Refinement

The number of hull shapes observed around the world is amazing. For a given length, hulls will have widely varying beams, draughts and displacements. The length of bow and stern overhangs along with deadrise angles and shear lines give unique character to a hull. These features are silently reflected in some of the measurements described previously: centre of buoyancy, centre of gravity, centre of floatation and displacement-to-length ratio.

Beam

A displacement hull's length is dictated by the required load-carrying ability. Determining the beam involves juggling different considerations. Wide beams increase the wave-making characteristic of the hull as well as the wetted surface. Increased wetted surface increases drag. However, beam does contribute considerably to the vessel's stability so balancing drag and stability is dependent on the seaworthiness requirements and application. Modern sailboats for example, require wide beams because they allow them to carry more sail and reduce heel. Low heel angles are required to allow the keel or centreboard to work efficiently. At high angles of heel, eddies are produced on the lee side of the keel which cause the boat to slip leeward. This leeway reduces the sailboat's ability to point upwind. Wide, flat deadrise sections abaft greatly improve sailing performance downwind. The shape resists rolling and allows the hull to approach semi-displacement S/L ratios because the beamy stern resists squatting. Therefore, the increased resistance of the wide beam is easily offset by improved upwind and downwind hull performance along with its ability to fly more sail area.

Unfortunately, excess stability produced by the beam generates a harsh rolling ride, especially in beam seas – a fact proved to many experienced seamen on beamy Platform Supply Vessels. However, the rolling characteristics of the hull are not strictly dependent on the beam; the cross-sectional shape of the hull is another key factor affecting seaworthiness and comfort. On hard-bilged, flat deadrise, U-shaped sections common in boat construction, wide beams will indeed produce harsh stability in seaway. However, a round section such as seen in whitewater canoes or trees, will be tender regardless of its beam.

On ships, beam is often dictated by the available widths of canals, dry docks and slips. Panamax ships for example are designed to be the largest volume (LOA, beam and draught) that will fit through the Panama Canal.

Displacement and Deadrise

A low centre of gravity is another method of achieving stability without increasing beam. A narrow beam generally gives a more comfortable ride. However, if the beam is very narrow it will respond too quickly to wind gust and shifting crew weight. Although stable, it will be uncomfortably tender. The most seaworthy hulls will have the stability gradually increase as one side is driven down by wave action or wind force. That is, the hull will not quickly recover from every wave-induced roll. This means that the boat will have steep deadrise, gradual turn of the bilge and flared freeboard. Moreover, it will have a low centre of gravity. These features all combine to make the hull self-righting which does not occur with some U-shaped hull designs.

Overhangs

The bow and stern overhangs of a vessel give boats their defining look. The stout double-ender looks as if it can take the worst the seas have to offer. Clipper bows reflect elegant yachting, straight bows and vertical transoms connote a mass-produced boat. Setting aside aesthetic discussions associated with over-hangs, shear lines, superstructure and the like, let us consider how overhangs affect boat performance.

The overhangs of the bow and stern will affect how the hull will handle waves. Their function is to offer reserve buoyancy that prevents the hull from ploughing into waves due to the inertia of the boat. As the bow is driven into a wave, the bow buoyancy increases quickly and the bow lifts out of the wave. The same is true at the stern. A full bow and stern, with little taper, has a similar effect. The advantage of overhang compared to full beamed bows and sterns is that 1) overhangs do not contribute to drag when not engaged by waves and 2) they provide a longer moment arm to the centre of floatation and therefore require less buoyancy for a given corrective moment. In practice, the overhangs of small craft are also accompanied by a sheerline that raises up at the bow to increase the freeboard at the bow. This balances the finer beam at the bow with additional reserve buoyancy developed by the higher freeboard.

To illustrate the importance of the over-hangs, consider the worst combination of overhangs. The worst combination would be to have little overhang at the bow and a lot at the stern. Assume following seas and a wave approaches astern. In response to the wave, the stern quickly lifts up the wave, driving the bow down. The bow, with little reserve buoyancy, readily drives into the water. This action gives a very wet ride at best and a catastrophic pitch-poling at worst. When surfing down the face of a large wave, we learn to quickly appreciate the reserve buoyancy provided by the bow. The opposite condition, that is a long bow overhang and short stern overhang is not at all attractive either. With an approaching wave, the bow lifts completely out of a wave due to the large reserve buoyancy provided by the overhung bow. The stern, with little reserve buoyancy, gets driven down into the water. When wave spacing is correct, the stern will get pooped. Because the overhangs do the work of maintaining trim in heavy seas, the stresses they encounter above the LWL and on the deck are very high.

Bow and stern overhang must be moderated to an extent. Too much overhang will give a very bumpy ride as the hull and stern pitch the boat in prompt response to the waves. This is the same behaviour that occurs athwartship when excess stability from the section shape causes the boat to roll quickly. With excess overhang, the bow and stern will lift too quickly in response to wave action. Therefore, the amount of overhang needs to be reduced to a point where it produces a safe, dry and smooth ride. In addition, as the vessel weight is decreased, the inertia is decreased and therefore the overhang requirement declines.

When speed is the only consideration, overhangs reduce speed. They do not contribute to the LWL that increases maximum displacement speed, but only add weight. Therefore, overhangs are either eliminated or reversed. Straight bows and reverse transoms are all that will show on a serious racing sailboat hull.

Sometimes hull refinements reflect the needs of local mariners. Many vessels in Asia, for example, must get through surf across undredged inlets before they can get to their fishing grounds. Therefore, they have very broad sterns so they can have shallow drafts. Surf boats will often have upswept bows to cut through the surf and prevent the flooding of the boat.

It is also worth mentioning that canoe-shaped sterns will allow for more manoeuvrability in following seas than a flat transom. When wide, flat transoms are hit by following seas, they can cause the boat to yaw uncontrollably.

Another subtle hull refinement applies to planing hulls. Planing hulls are designed around features that produce hydrodynamic lift. They generally have a very fine entrance and flat bottom as described previously. The hulls will often have a series of lifting strakes running longitudinally along the bottom of the hull near the turn of the bilge. The strakes

---

Summary of Hull Features

Seaworthy Hull

    Low centre of gravity
    Moderate deadrise
    Moderate beam
    Good bow overhang and fullness
    Moderate stern overhang
    Heavy displacement
    Moderate freeboard

Fast Hull

    Wide beam
    Extra beam at stern
    Fine bow
    Little overhang, reverse stern shear
    Light displacement
    Zero deadrise, hard bilges
    Low freeboard and smooth hull (reduces
      aerodynamic drag)

are small protrusions that give additional horizontal surfaces for planing and improve directional stability. Planing hulls will also have a greater topside flare to direct the spray outward and keep the decks drier.

The following list of hull characteristics summarises features found in seaworthy and fast hulls. This list does not include all the other factors that go into making a vessel seaworthy as opposed to fast. Such things as the hull, deck and superstructure's strength along with the design of the bilge pump system, hatches, scuppers and redundant systems have a direct relationship to seaworthiness. Higher propulsive power with a low weight obviously provides higher speed. High-speed boats also benefit from sleek superstructure and hull features that minimize aerodynamic drag.

Sailboat Keels

Three-quarters of the wind's force is used to drive a close-hauled sailboat sideways, with only a quarter used to propel the boat forwards. Therefore, keels or leeboards have long been used on sailing craft to resist leeway movement. When the British 'six beamers' started using external ballast, the keel assumed the dual role of holding the external ballast as far away from the metacentre as possible and preventing leeway. Moreover, keels have the tertiary role of accepting the impact of groundings.

The keel has a challenging existence. It experiences high athwartship stresses under normal sailing conditions yet it must be very thin to keep drag low. This thinness does not allow the athwartship moment of inertia to be high; therefore, the keel must obtain its strength by brute force. The keel is also subject to high longitudinal and vertical stresses caused by groundings. All these stresses are transmitted to the hull and this is the reason that the keel connection is so critical. In addition to the high strength required

of the keel, it is important that it be well streamlined and smooth because it travels entirely submerged in clean, unaerated water. Smooth flowing, unaerated water is the most sensitive to surface friction because of the higher viscosity of water as opposed to air.

A short underwater profile gives a boat faster response to the rudder. On the other hand, long surfaces provide more steady, directionally stable motion but at the expense of increased drag. On sailboats this translates to the performance advantage of the long, thin fin keel versus a full keel that runs the entire length of the vessel. Deep, slender fin keels produce less friction drag. They also produce weaker, energy-consuming vortices off the narrower tip. Long keels give better longitudinal stability and shallower draught but suffer from increased drag.

The ideal keel shape would be very long and slender with a slight sweepback and taper towards the bottom. It would be winged with radii at the bottom of each wing. All the weight would be held at the very end of the keel. However, the practicalities of hauling the vessel out and groundings, not to mention construction costs, modify the meaning of ideal. Flat-bottomed, straight keels are easier to store and manufacture. In addition, draught is a key consideration for many mariners. Therefore, shallow draught requirements often dictate the keel design.

Structure

Boats are basically made with a skin attached to a framework consisting of longitudinal stringers and athwartship bulkheads (or frames). The stringers give longitudinal strength, preventing the hull from flexing up and down along its keel. Bulkheads resist hull twisting. Both the bulkheads and stringers are integrated to provide a strong hull. The bulkheads support the stringers and the stringers support the bulkhead. Bulkheads are used not only for stiffness but also for reserve watertightness. This type of egg-crate construction has been used on the relatively small Chinese junks from before Marco Polo first commented on this design in 1298. He noted that the bulkheads protected the boat from sinking 'if she springs a leak by running against a rock, or on being hit by a hungry whale'.

Water leaks are often signs of inadequate framing or excessive flexibility. For example, a porthole is a hard point on a hull and if the hull constantly flexes around the porthole, it will always leak. Chronic leakage usually indicates insufficient bulkheading. Bulkheads are often compromised by access or lightening holes. When holes need to be cut into a structural member, they should be done near its neutral axis where the stress is lowest. Putting holes towards the outside of a member weakens it tremendously (see the 'Primer on Composite Materials' for a discussion of the effect of location on the moment of inertia).

Bulkheads are principally responsible for preventing hull twisting whereas stringers provide longitudinal strength. Together with frames, these features maintain hull rigidity. Although some hull flexibility is acceptable, the drive train must be very rigid, otherwise the engine, gear, shaft and strut will be damaged.

The deck is part of the structural support for most offshore craft. An inadequately supported deck weakens the vessel and excess flexibility will produce chronic water leakage just as a hull does. Water leaks are a good tell-tale sign for weak designs. The superstructure also needs to be adequately supported. Some designers basically rely on the rigidity of the cabin's window frames to support flying bridges or will put large windows in flexible sections. Unless run at dead slow in calm weather, these windows will always leak.

Bulkheads and stringers are notoriously weakened by clearance notches and access holes. Both of these disfigurements not only lower the moment of inertia but also provide sources of stress concentrations. Stringers should be continuous runs that are tightly bound to the framework and the skin, whether it be FRP, metal or wood.

Manufacturing Techniques

The building of boats is an ancient craft. Knowledge of wood characteristics in a marine setting was vital. The temptation to make heavy, strong boats had to be moderated by the practical necessity of keeping them light and flexible – not to mention the tremendous effort it took to produce planks from trees.

Light planking over a strong framework was the basis for boat building until the age of FRP construction. Boat materials have evolved from wood to iron to steel to aluminium and finally to FRP. Of course steel and aluminium are still common and have many advantages. Building boats from wood will probably always be a cherished endeavour, and in many cases, wood is the only affordable material. Only iron, bark, animal skins and the like have fallen out of fashion.

Metal and wood boat construction is usually started by lofting, or drawing, the full size shapes of pieces that make up the boat. Templates may be made to guide the cutting of the material or the material may be directly cut with computer guidance based on the boat plans. FRP construction relies on a mould to obtain the desired shape.

FRP

Wet layup is the oldest technique used to make FRP boats. In this process, a waxy mould release agent is first applied to the inside of a female mould. The release agent prevents the hull from sticking to the mould as oil does in a cooking pan. Gel coat (for example, isophthalic neopentyl glycol) is then painted on the inside of a mould. The gel coat carries the boat's colour and produces a very thin, shiny, smooth watertight surface. Sometimes another watertight layer is added under the gel coat (for example a bisphenolic resin) to improve the sealing of the underlying laminates. Next, fibres are laid on top of the gel coat surface inside the mould. The orientation and fibre density applied varies depending on the loads anticipated and the manufacturer's preference. Cloth is the most tightly woven form of fibre, having the highest density of fibre packing in any two-dimensional form. Consequently, it is the strongest but it is also the heaviest fibre composition. It is often used on the inner and outer layers of the laminate where the stresses are the highest. Filler fibres are used to build up most of the FRP thickness. These consist of woven roving and mat. The woven roving is a lighter weave than the cloth and is much thicker. Mat is an even looser composition of randomly oriented fibres. Mat has nearly equal strength in all three dimensions because of the random orientation of the fibres. Mat can be obtained in thicknesses up to 0.06 in (1.5 mm) and is the fastest way to build up thickness.

Unidirectional fibres, or rovings in their bundled form, are the best fibre composition for gaining high strength. These rovings have fibres lying in the same direction as opposed to the two or three-dimensional weaves discussed previously. These can be used to reinforce highly stressed sections or run diagonally to reduce hull flexure.

As each layer of fibre is applied to the mould, a carefully controlled amount of resin is applied to the fibre by an impregnator. An impregnator is a tool that meters out the resin between a set of rollers. Alternatively, the fibres can be 'wetted out' by brushing or rolling resin over the fibres by hand. A release fabric is laid on top of the wetted fibres and then the whole assembly is squeegeed to remove excess resin. Once the entire surface of the fibres is wetted by resin, it is important to remove as much of the resin as possible because excess resin adds weight and expense without providing additional strength.

Coring is used to provide sandwich construction. This provides a strong, rigid panel (see 'Primer on Composite Materials') and also makes the boat quieter and provides thermal insulation. The coring is bonded to the outside FRP layers. The coring must be flexible enough to follow the curves of the hull. Typically core sheets are used. These sheets consist of small squares attached to a cloth sheet. It is in this manner that edge-grained balsa can be used. The balsa blocks are attached to the sheet so that their grains are perpendicular to the sheet. Consequently, because wood is stronger in the direction of its grain, this end grain orientation provides the strongest resistance to crushing. Moreover, water will not migrate readily between the grains. Polymeric foams and honeycombs are becoming much more popular in sandwich construction. These may be obtained in easy to use flexible sheets.

Vacuum bagging is an improved FRP technique. In this technique a sealed bag is placed around the mould and layup. A vacuum pump draws a vacuum in the bag, allowing external air pressure to uniformly squeeze the assembly. This is especially important in sandwich construction to ensure good core bonding.

Advanced composites (carbon and Kevlar) are usually worked in 'pre-preg' form which are prepared sheets or tapes of fibres impregnated with a controlled amount of resin. They are worked just like dry reinforcements but the pre-preg must be heated up to activate the resin. Pre-pregs are the best way to work with composites because they ensure the consistency of the composite's strength. They are carefully manufactured to completely and evenly coat the fibres as well as remove air voids. Pre-pregs can be processed to allow different stickiness (tack) and flexibility (drape) to facilitate handling during the layup process. They have a limited shelf life and lend themselves to large manufacturing operations.

Composite construction techniques and materials rapidly change. The development of resins is especially dynamic and is hard to keep up with. The underpinnings of composite materials probably will not change. Entrained air in the resin, poor wetting of the fibres, poor core bonding, fatigue and heat damage are among the problems that will probably remain after the term for glue has been replaced by exotic, polysyllabic words.

Steel, Aluminium and Wood

Steel, aluminium and wooden boats are constructed in very similar ways. In fact, the first 'composite' boats were made by using wooden planks on iron frames. Although there are a variety of construction methods, the following outlines the basic approach to constructing boats from steel, aluminium or wood.

First the keel, stem and stern are assembled.

After this step, a series of curved ribs or frames are attached to the keel. The ribs are then tied together by longitudinal stringers that curve to the shape of the hull. Separate beams attached to the top of the ribs are used to produce the strong box-like frame of the hull. These beams also support the deck. Athwartship bulkheads are added for additional strength and on larger craft, provide watertight compartments for reserve damage buoyancy. Larger craft will often have longitudinal bulkheads as well.

The vessel's skin is attached to the outside of the frame. In wooden vessels it consists of a number of horizontal planks. Planking is usually set end to end with caulking between the planks. This carvel construction gives a smooth surface. The planks can be laid in an overlapping fashion, called lapstrake or clinker planking. Double-planked boats are common in larger wooden boats. In this case, the inner set of planking is usually run diagonally and the outer layer is horizontal.

Propeller Design and Application Guide

A propeller, or screw, is a helix that is driven through the water. A propeller's performance is measured by its efficiency. The shape and condition of a propeller is very important. Because propellers operate at a much higher speed than the hull, their streamlined shape and smoothness strongly affect their efficiency. Corrosion cavitation or impact damage will greatly increase the frictional drag. If these conditions occur at the leading edge, or to a lesser degree the trailing edge, the pressure drag also increases. The condition of the propeller is so critical for efficient propulsion that the *Queen Elizabeth II* saved US$7,000 of fuel per day due to improved efficiency when she had both of her five-bladed propellers polished a few years ago.

A propeller's *geometric pitch* is the length of advance provided by one turn of the propeller if it does not slip in the water. Unfortunately, a rotating propeller slips backward through the water and this actual advance through the water in one revolution is called the *effective pitch*. The difference between the geometric pitch and effective pitch is appropriately called *slip*. The geometric pitch specified for a vessel is dependent on the power and desired operating speed of the vessel. Propeller efficiency is related to the slip but is actually the ratio of generated propulsion versus energy required to rotate the propeller. Marine propellers are usually 50 per cent efficient.

Propeller speed, diameter and pitch are based on the displacement, operating speed, engine power, hull design and number of propellers desired. Given these factors, the propeller needs to be sized to match the optimal operating speed of the engine/gear combination.

There are a variety of propeller designs. The most basic delineation of propeller designs is based on the number of blades they carry. Generally, two-bladed propellers with high pitch-to-diameter ratios are used for high-speed boats. For lower speeds a three-blade propeller with a pitch-diameter ratio of approximately 1.0 is the most efficient. For boats operating at low speeds and requiring high thrust, such as workboats, a four-blade propeller with low pitch-diameter ratios provide the highest propeller efficiency. Four-bladed propellers are often used to replace three-bladed propellers when improved acceleration, manoeuvrability and a smoother ride are desired. Five-bladed propellers are used on larger craft or when needed to reduce excessive vibration.

Selecting the correct propeller is not only important for optimal speed and thrust but also to ensure engine durability. Too small a propeller pitch will cause excessive propeller shaft speed. This excessive speed will increase engine and gear wear. Conversely, the engine speed may run below its designed operating speed if the engine is overloaded by driving a propeller with too large a diameter or pitch. This overloading can result in excessive carbon build-up in the cylinder with subsequent problems of poor fuel economy, scoring of the cylinder walls and even burned pistons. On petrol engines, overloading may also frequently foul the spark plugs.

The following rules of thumb provide guidance on propeller clearance and usage:

Displacement Hull

Propeller tip clearance:	10% of wheel diameter
Propeller rpm:	300 – 900
Propeller pitch/diameter ratio:	0.5 – 0.9
Slip	30 – 40% (up to 80% for tug and tow boats)

Semi-displacement Hull

Propeller tip clearance:	10% of wheel diameter
Propeller rpm:	800 – 1800
Propeller pitch/diameter ratio:	0.8 – 1.1
Slip	25 – 35 %

Planing Hull

Propeller tip clearance:	15% of wheel diameter for single screw, 12% for twin screws
Propeller rpm:	1,000 – 3,000
Propeller pitch/diameter ratio:	0.9 – 1.4
Slip	10 – 35%

Vessels intended for low speed towing or pushing nearly always employ a ducted propeller system. This system simply wraps a nozzle (sometimes referred to as a Kort nozzle) around the propeller to reduce losses from water flowing axially out from the propeller tips and wasting thrust. These nozzles can increase low speed thrust up to 55 per cent and up to 25 per cent at trawling speeds. They are therefore commonly seen on tugs, pushboats, trawlers, draggers and other vessels that pull heavy loads.

The ideal propeller shape is modified to accommodate practical concerns. For example, many propellers have overly thick leading edges to resist impact damage. The blade is also more gradually transitioned into the hub than an ideal propeller. This is done to reduce stress concentrations and account for machining capabilities.

Folding, cupped edge, contrarotating, variable pitch, surface piercing and super-cavitating propellers are among the speciality propellers that meet the needs of sailing yachts and fast craft. A folding propeller is a two-blade propeller designed to allow the blades to fold back in line with the propeller shaft. These are used on sailboats to reduce drag when under sail. Cupped edge propellers are used to reduce slip at high propeller speeds. They can provide another couple of knots of speed and reduce cavitation. Contrarotating propellers have two propellers in the same plane with the aft propeller being driven by the forward propeller. This design eliminates the wasted torqueing energy of the propeller and increases propeller efficiency. Variable pitch propellers can have the pitch changed while underway. These are used on high-speed craft that need to modify the pitch to provide optimal high-speed performance. Surface piercing propellers reduce propeller-induced drag by allowing one blade to penetrate the surface and rotate in the air. Because air has a lower viscosity than water, this reduces drag. Super-cavitating propellers are designed to have the back of the propeller blade completely cavitated. They can run at very high propeller speeds because the pressure on the cavitated back of the blade will not decrease with increased propeller speed, yet the thrust will continue to rise with increased speed. This design is used on some racing boats.

Fastener Design and Application Guide

The delicate wisps of material that bond great objects hardly look up to their task. They are called upon to hold with their eagle's claw, large plates of steel, aluminium, fibreglass and other powerful materials. What started as hardwood dowels and wooden lace have evolved into the ubiquitous bolt and rivet. Bolts along with the whole family of commercially available threaded fasteners range from unregulated cosmetic bolts to hold trim pieces, to high quality, carefully machined 'Jesus' nuts used on helicopters to attach the rotor.

Welding

Reliably welded steel plates allowed the proliferation of Liberty ships – 2,700 ships built in four years during the Second World War. Welds eliminated the weight and drag of the heavy rivets used at the start of the century. Ships have been welded since as early as 1920 but the technique did not completely take over steel construction until after the Second World War and the experience gained by Liberty ship construction.

Welding is the process of joining two metal objects by melting the materials and fusing them together. The parts to be welded are rigidly held by clamps. It is common for parts to move as they are heated and cooled, and an experienced welder will shim parts in anticipation of their movement. It is also common

practice to tack weld (a very small temporary weld) an object to develop the general shape. After the part is in its final shape, continuous welds are made to produce the final object. Residual stresses can linger in these welded joints after the clamps are removed; therefore, welds are often heat-treated to remove these stresses. Large panels or repetitive welding processes are usually done by robotic or automated welders.

Both material strength and fatigue life is lower in the weld than the original unwelded material. This is due to metallurgical changes developed by the high welding temperatures, the shape of the weld, voids and operator error. Generally, the maximum stress allowed in the weld is between 40 to 66 per cent of the yield stress of the filler metal, depending on the type of loading. Fatigue strength also is reduced in the weld. The fatigue strength is reduced from 15 per cent for a butt weld to 60 per cent at the end of certain fillet welds.

The two most common welded joints are fillet or butt welds. These welds lay a bead of filler material either at the apex of a joint, in the case of a fillet weld, or at the ends of two materials in the case of the butt weld. Resistance welding, such as spot welding, is the cheapest welding technique. The weld is made simply by passing an electrical current through the parts to be welded. This current melts the material and produces the weld; this technique eliminates the need for filler rods and fluxes. However, spot welding can only be used on thin sheets. The heat-affected zone around these welds is difficult to control and they are not good in tension. A common failure mechanism occurs in spot welds when the hardened weld area tears out under tension.

Threaded Fasteners

Threaded fasteners describe parts that employ a thread to develop clamping force. Screws and bolts are the most commonly used threaded fasteners. The difference between a screw and a bolt is that a bolt is tightened with a nut whereas a screw is engaged into a tapped hole and is tightened by torqueing its head. Machine screws (which are often used as bolts) are small screws whereas cap screws are large screws. Bolts are fastened by using a washer, lockwasher and nut or simply a washer and a locking-style nut (e.g. Nylok). Both screws and bolts benefit from thread lubrication not only for corrosion resistance but also to prevent any loosening of their preload clamping force. Preload is the force produced by tightening the fastener.

Although it sounds contrary, a high preload on the fastener is beneficial, especially in terms of improving the fatigue strength of the bolt. The preload is important because it reduces the range of stresses that the fastener will experience. Because the preload is much higher than the load that the joint would normally encounter, the relatively small stresses that are added or subtracted from the bolt do not vary much from its average value. This is a highly desirable condition because this low ratio of maximum stress to average stress means excellent fatigue strength.

A high preload also reduces the shearing force by drawing the two fastened materials tightly together. This increases the frictional force that is in direct relation to the perpendicular clamping force provided by the fastener. The preload torque should produce about 90 per cent of the *proof load*. Proof load is basically the same as maximum yield load but is a term used in the fastener industry to describe the maximum tensile force a fastener can handle without yielding. The toughest load a threaded fastener should ever experience is its initial tightening. If it does not break during tightening, it should never break in service if it does not corrode.

Although 90 per cent seems high, a part of this preload overcomes the friction of the bolt/nut/material interfaces. Preloading also creates a twisting, torsional stress in the fastener. However, once the tightening torque is removed, the torsional stress disappears as high points and dirt are flattened out. With bolted fasteners that do not move at all, it is sometimes helpful to back the nut a 1/8 turn to eliminate excessive torsional stress. It is also worth mentioning that rivet behaviour

Recommended Minimum Torque Values (ft-lbs)

SAE Grade	Metric Grade	Bolt Diameter (inches)									
		1/4	5/16	3/8	7/16	1/2	9/16	5/8	3/4	7/8	1
1	4.6	3	6	11	18	28	43	55	97	155	230
2	5.8	5	10	18	30	47	72	91	160	155	230
3		8	16	28	46	70	105	130			
5	8.8	8	16	28	46	70	110	140	250	405	600
7		10	21	35	56	85	140	170	310	495	745
8	10.9	11	23	40	65	99	159	198	350	566	848

is basically the same as that of bolts, only the means of securing and preloading rivets are different.

A torque wrench is the best way to verify preload. However, the 'turn of the nut' method is also a good technique. The number of turns after hand tightening is specified with this method rather than specifying a torque. The number of turns relates directly to the preload value.

Shaft and Terminal Fasteners

Keys, pins, clips and cotter pins form another category of fasteners commonly used on rotating objects such as gears and pulleys as well as for securing terminals. Usually the width of the key is 1/4 the shaft diameter and the length is based on the required strength.

The cutting of the keyway will produce a stress concentration. This stress concentration factor for keyways produced by common manufacturing techniques usually ranges from 1.4 – 1.8. There are a variety of clips in service. Most of them are made from hardened spring steel and are intended to engage a shaft slot to hold the shaft in position.

Bonded Joints

A bonded joint is made by using a separate material to attach two objects as is done with brazing, soldering and gluing. Sandwich construction, which uses resin adhesion to bond a core and composite laminate, is an example of a bonded joint. Plywood is another common example of a bonded joint.

Cracked welds are very common. This weld was used to repair a damaged transom. The weld bonded well to the transom but eventually cracked right down the middle. The nearby bracket is a protective bar for a jet drive. The original damage to the transom was probably caused by it backing into a pier.

Pump Design and Application Guide

One of the first things passed over to a floundering boat is a self-contained bilge pump. Pumps have kept boats afloat for years and one has to believe that after the first mariner launched his boat, he fashioned a pump or bailer to keep it afloat. From the simple pail to modern, high capacity, centrifugal pumps, bilge pumps have kept up with the demands presented by torrential rains, breaking waves and leaky hulls.

At least 3,000 years ago someone looked at flowing water and thought up the waterwheel – the world's first mechanical pump. The person that first devised this idea was, of course, laden with pumps of his own – the heart being the most renowned. Archimedes' screw pump was invented over 2,000 years ago. Both the waterwheel and the screw pump (commonly used in the form of a progressive cavity pump that will move anything from coal slurry to fish heads) are still used.

The most heroic use of pumps on boats is as bilge pumps. Pumps are also used on almost all mechanical systems such as in the fuel, lubricating oil, engine coolant, hydraulic, refrigeration, potable water and sanitation systems. Pumps are considered turbomachinery, *turbo* being the Latin word for spin. If a machine adds energy to a fluid it is called a *pump*, if it depletes the energy it is called a *turbine*. In fact, pumps can inadvertently be turned into turbines just as their electrical cousins, motors, can be turned into generators.

Although the semantics are interesting, in common usage not all pumps spin and pumps are specifically referred to as machines that add energy to liquids. If gases are pumped, the pump is called a fan, blower or compressor. These terms are simply delineated by the pressure they produce; fans produce up to 1 psig (0.069 bar), blowers 1 – 25 psig (0.069 – 1.72 bar), and compressors over 25 psig (1.72 bar). Pressure in English units are referred to as either psia (pounds per square inch, absolute) and psig (pounds per square inch, gauge). Psia is the pressure of a fluid including that produced by the gravitational force on our atmosphere. At sea level the column of air above us exerts 14.7 psi. Psig is the pressure measured relative to the atmospheric pressure. Therefore, psia is simply psig plus 14.7 psi. These problems are avoided by using units of either atmosphere or bar. One atmosphere and one bar are equal to the weight of the atmosphere at sea level or 14.7 psia. When psi alone is used it is usually in reference to a pressure change. However, it is common practice to call psig simply psi.

There are two categories of pumps: dynamic and positive displacement. Positive displacement pumps force the fluid to move by shear mechanical force and move a fixed volume of fluid each cycle. They work by opening a chamber and drawing fluid in. The inlet is then closed and an outlet is opened. Mechanical force pushes the fluid out. Dynamic pumps, on the other hand, work by increasing the velocity of the fluid and 'throwing' it out of the discharge. The centrifugal pump is the most common example of this type.

Positive displacement pumps seem easier to understand and have many advantages. However, dynamic pumps are extremely popular in the form of centrifugal pumps and have uniquely attractive characteristics of their own.

Differences between Centrifugal Pumps and Positive Displacement Pumps

Advantages of Centrifugal Pumps over Positive Displacement Pumps
  1. High efficiency
      Produce higher flow per unit of power and, consequently, higher flow-to-weight ratio.

  2. Smooth flow
      Produce smooth, non-pulsating discharge, like the flow from a water tap.

  3. Long life
      The only solid-to-solid contact in a dynamic pump is at the shaft bearing; therefore, they experience less wear than a positive displacement pump.

  4. Quieter
      Produce a pleasant 'whirring' sound rather than the banging sound of most positive displacement pumps.

Advantages of Positive Displacement Pumps over Dynamic Pumps
  1. Handle particulates
      The ability to handle solid particles

varies tremendously by the specific design. Centrifugal pumps can handle small particulates but it shortens their durability.

  2. Flow rate is independent of flow restrictions
      The pressure will decrease but the flow rate stays constant. The discharge rate of centrifugal pumps drops quickly with increasing flow restriction.

  3. Flow rate is independent of viscosity
      For example, oil is more viscous when it is cold and a positive displacement pump will continue to deliver the same flow rate regardless of the oil's temperature and subsequent viscosity.

  4. Self-priming and can draw a vacuum
      Self-priming means that the positive displacement pump can draw fluid from a tank that lies below the inlet of the pump. Centrifugal pumps usually need to be primed and generally cannot draw fluid by vacuum to the inlet. Rather, the fluid must flood the pump inlet.

  5. High pressure
      Positive displacement pumps can generally develop higher pressure at lower flow rates than centrifugal pumps. Piston pumps are commonly used to obtain pressures of 3,000 psi (20 MPa).

Positive displacement pumps are usually selected where high pressures at low flow rates are required. They are also used where flow rates must be maintained regardless of pressure, or when the pump must be completely self-priming or handle dirty fluids. These are very broad statements and there are many exceptions, for example, centrifugal pumps can be self-priming and can handle reasonably dirty fluids.

The following outlines some of the different pump designs and their classifications:

Pump Classifications

Positive Displacement Pumps

1. Reciprocating
   a) Diaphragm
   b) Piston
   c) Plunger

2. Rotary
   a) Sliding vane
   b) Peristaltic
   c) Gear
   d) Lobe
   e) Screw

Dynamic Pumps
   a) Centrifugal
   b) Axial flow (propeller)
   c) Jet
   d) Fluid activated

In many ways, positive displacement pumps are the easiest to understand. Our bodies are full of these pumps from our hearts to our diaphragms. Reciprocating pumps, for example, simply use a tube with a piston drawn through its centre. The piston is pulled up from one end, which creates a vacuum on the opposite end. This vacuum draws up the liquid. In practice, a suction and discharge valve are alternately opened and closed to produce flow. This is the same principle we use to suck water through a straw. When our diaphragm moves down, it creates a vacuum all the way to our mouths and, in turn, the straw. As atmospheric pressure works on all the water around the straw, the water is drawn into our mouths. The popular diaphragm pump is a reciprocating-type pump that works on this principle of a diaphragm moving in and out to draw and dispel liquid.

Rotary pumps rotate a gear or impeller within a casing to move a fluid, acting much like a rotating paddlewheel does in propelling a boat. Vane pumps, flexible impeller pumps and gear pumps are of this type. Peristaltic pumps use a flexible tube that is squeezed by a rotating roller to move the liquid through the tube. It works in the same way that fingers can squeeze out an air bubble from under plastic tape. A sliding vane motor uses an eccentrically mounted rotor that holds sliding vanes within a cylinder. As the rotor is driven, the vanes encapsulating a large space are forced inward by the pressure of the cylinder and increase the fluid pressure. Pneumatic equipment often use sliding vane 'pumps' as motors. Compressed air enters the pump and the expanding force of the air causes the rotor to turn.

Centrifugal pumps are the most important member of the dynamic pump family. The centrifugal pump consists of a paddlewheel-like impeller contained within a casing. It differs from a positive displacement pump in that the impeller does not contact the casing – fluid can flow completely through the pump, either forwards or backwards, when the impeller is not turning.

Fluid enters the pump in the centre through the casing where it is caught by the rotating impeller and thrown outwards into the outer casing. This outer casing or *scroll* gives the centrifugal pump its distinctive doughnut-like shape and provides an area where the discharged fluid can expand, slow down and increase pressure. Dynamic pumps are important to the marine surveyor, not just because of the centrifugal pump but rather its close cousin the propeller. Propellers are simply a variant of the centrifugal pump.

Cavitation is a familiar event in propellers but it also occurs in any rotating pump. It is caused when the vacuum produced falls below the vapour pressure or boiling point of the fluid. The boiling point is the temperature at a particular pressure (sea level is its most commonly used reference pressure). As the pressure decreases, the boiling temperature also decreases. This is why water boils at a lower temperature at high altitudes and food that requires boiling must be boiled longer to offset the lower temperature. In the case of cavitation, the pressure developed behind the propeller is so low that the fluid boils at the ambient temperature. During cavitation, the fluid boils and collapses. This action abrades the object that produced the low pressure, such as propellers and impellers. The damage caused by the boiling can occur at pressures below the boiling point of the liquid due to dissolved gases or lighter fluids boiling out first.

The inlet pressure required to prevent cavitation is available for each pump design. This value is called the net positive-suction head (NPSH). The term 'head' is synonymous with pressure and draws an image of the force of water held above an object. The net positive-suction head is dependent on the pressure and velocity of the pump outlet and the vapour pressure of the liquid. Commonly, centrifugal pumps require a 'flooded suction'. This means that the inlet of the pump is always completely full of fluid but no additional inlet pressure is required. As higher and higher pressures are required, more stages are added to the centrifugal pump; the first stage raises the pressure to drive the second stage which in turn drives the third stage and so on. In this manner, high pressures can be achieved with a centrifugal pump with a low inlet pressure and still not produce destructive cavitation.

Engine Systems Design and Application Guide

Engine Cooling Systems

The best way to maximise engine damage is to disable the coolant system. As the engine temperature gradually rises all sort of parts seize, melt or otherwise get damaged before the engine stops working and generating the destructive heat. It is for this reason the military has experimented with ceramic-based 'adiabatic' engines that do not require any cooling.

Cooling systems are divided into two categories, open loop and closed loop. Open loop cooling systems simply draw in raw water and circulate it through the engine cooling system. This system's simplicity is offset by its dependence on unconstrained, clean and non-corrosive water. Consequently, sea-going vessels and workboats do not use open loop cooling. Closed loop cooling uses raw water to cool an engine coolant through a heat exchanger or keel cooler. This system allows the engine coolant to be maintained in a separate closed loop; therefore, expensive coolants with corrosion inhibitors and low freezing points can be maintained in the loop.

Heat Exchanger Cooling

A heat exchanger cooled system is a closed loop system that consists of a heat exchanger, suction pump and strainer. The vacuum produced by a suction pump draws the raw water into the system. The inlet of the pump has a strainer to prevent foreign material from clogging the pump or heat exchanger. The raw water is pumped into the heat exchanger. There, the raw water flows into a cluster of tubes that are immersed in a reservoir containing the engine coolant. The raw water that has been heated by this contact with the hot coolant is pumped overboard. The coolant that has been cooled is pumped back to the engine. An expansion tank is included in the coolant system to accommodate the change in coolant volume produced by different temperatures. A deaeration tank is also part of the cooling system and allows the air to separate from the coolant.

Design guidance for these systems will depend on the engine manufacturer but the following guidelines generally apply:

- The maximum pressure drop through the heat exchanger at full flow should be less than 5 psi (34 kPa).

- A self-priming pump is required for the raw water pump because the pump needs to prime itself each time the engine is turned on.

- The raw water suction through-hull must be mounted low and in a position that will assure that it is continuously flooded, even in heavy seas.

• The raw water strainer should be sized to strain particles over 0.06 in (1.6 mm).

• Ice and debris can block strainers; therefore, dual raw water suction through-hulls and strainers should be used where this problem is anticipated.

• Coolant temperature should be maintained at less than 200°F (93°C).

• The entire raw water system must have excellent corrosion protection. This is achieved by the correct specification of materials and sacrificial anodes (see 'Primer on Corrosion').

• The cooling systems for multiple engines should be combined at the heat exchanger and not from a tee connection in the coolant lines.

Air needs to be eliminated from the cooling system because it can accelerate corrosion in coolant passages and increase coolant expansion. The deaerator taps off a small portion of the coolant and allows it to reside in a non-turbulent area where the air can separate from the water. This deaerated water is then introduced back into the coolant through a make-up line.

The deaeraetor is normally part of the expansion tank and is made with a vented baffle plate. The expansion tank is a chamber that can accommodate the approximately five per cent increase in coolant volume that normally occurs as the coolant heats up to engine temperature. The expansion tank is sized somewhat larger than what is required for thermal expansion. This gives reserve to make up coolant lost from evaporation or leakage.

Because the air entrained in the coolant rises, the expansion tank is located at the high point of the entire coolant system. Vent lines are usually routed to the tank from the highest point in the engine coolant system and the highest point in the entire cooling system. Additional vent lines are located at the high point of the heat exchanger or keel cooler to allow the removal of air when they are initially filled with coolant. These lines must rise continuously to the expansion tank, as any loops will cause air traps.

The make-up line that reintroduces the deaerated coolant must flow from the bottom of the expansion tank to the coolant inlet line. In order to get good reintroduction of the deaerated coolant; it should not be plumbed directly into the pump inlet or near any bends or elbows. The flow from the make-up line should be equal to the flow from all the vent lines. Therefore, these lines must be sized appropriately.

Coolant temperature warning indicators or alarms must be installed. In addition to normal mechanical problems, a marine heat exchanger coolant system will often overheat due to blockage of the raw water strainer. The best warning system includes an early warning alarm and automatic shutdown in addition to a normal overheating alarm.

Keel Cooling

Keel cooling is used on boats working in water containing heavy silt, jellyfish or ice. Under these conditions, the suction strainers will quickly plug and the heat exchanger will be quickly abraded by silt. Keel cooling uses pipes or channels mounted on the outside of the hull and below the waterline. This becomes a large heat exchanger and engine coolant is circulated through the keel cooler to provide the necessary cooling. Keel coolers must be protected from damage due to docking or heavy debris. Keel coolers are sized based on the design boat speed and the efficiency of the cooler and are conservatively sized to allow decreased performance due to corrosion and marine growth.

Common design considerations for keel coolers are:

• The keel cooler should be located where it is not subject to pounding waves, hull flexing or excessive vibration.

• The keel cooler should be located well below

the waterline to avoid the aerated surface water. The best location is near the keel in the centre of the boat because this section is the stiffest.

• Slow-moving vessels should mount the keel cooler near the propeller to gain the benefit of the faster water flow in this region.

• Engine transmissions can usually use the engine cooling system although some manufacturers will recommend separate systems.

Engine Exhaust System

Engine exhaust is very hot and presents a fire and burning hazard. Moreover, engine exhaust gas contains dangerous carbon monoxide along with acid-forming chemicals and abrasive particulates. With all of these problems to handle, engine exhaust system design is vitally important. The exhaust system must convey the gases away from the boat without letting it leak into the boat. In addition, the system must not destroy itself by the powerful forces produced by thermal expansion. The system must also resist corrosive acids and abrasive particulates.

The two types of exhaust system encountered on boats are the wet and dry types. The wet exhaust system injects raw water to cool the exhaust. Consequently, the exhaust and exhaust piping are cooled and can be safely routed through the boat. The dry exhaust simply discharges the exhaust into the atmosphere through a silencer or muffler.

Regardless of whether the exhaust is the wet or dry type, the hot exhaust piping must have no leaks and be separated from wood, FRP or any other combustible material. Besides these safety factors, the other two important considerations in evaluating an exhaust system are thermal expansion and exhaust back-pressure. Back-pressure is any unwanted positive pressure in an area that should be at atmospheric pressure. Any obstruction in the exhaust system will produce undesirable back-pressure.

Obstructions can include any of the following exhaust line flow restrictions: tight or an excessive number of bends, undersize piping and incorrect muffler sizing. Obstructions will also decrease the power output and fuel efficiency of the engine. High back-pressure results in the incomplete expulsion of the exhaust gases from the cylinders. Consequently, the air-to-fuel ratio in the cylinders changes and the exhaust temperature will rise. Wet exhaust systems usually have a higher back-pressure because of the presence of steam in the system.

Because exhaust systems get very hot, special attention to the effect of thermal expansion must be considered. The systems must be sufficiently flexible to allow for thermal expansion yet rigid enough to handle engine vibrations without fatigue failure. These considerations are especially important in dry exhausts where long lengths of hot pipe are used. These performance requirements are usually handled by using a flexible link or by allowing the expansion of rigid pipe by flexible pipe supports.

When inspecting an exhaust system at room temperature, remember that a 15 ft steel pipe will expand one inch (five metres gives 28 mm of expansion) in length under normal engine operation. To address thermal expansion, short runs of exhaust pipe can simply have one end of the pipe anchored and the other end free so that it can move out as the pipe expands. However, a flexible exhaust connection is normally required by the engine manufacturer to absolutely protect the exhaust manifold or turbocharger from thermally-induced stress. The flexible connection also prevents the transmission of engine vibrations to the exhaust system.

Long horizontal and vertical piping should have flexible connections. The flexible connections should always run straight because a bend will greatly increase the exhaust impingement on the obstructing side and shorten its life. When the flexible connection is cold it should have sufficient room to compress as it heats. A flexible connection that is installed completely compressed on a cold exhaust is useless.

A combination of vertical and horizontal connections produces the best design because it gives the system flexibility. Moreover, it allows the inclusion of a condensation trap and drain. This allows soot and acid-laden exhaust condensate to collect in the trap rather than flowing back into the engine. With this same consideration of acidic condensate, horizontal flexible connections upstream of vertical runs should be installed as far away as possible from the vertical run. This location reduces the amount of soot and acid collected in the bellows of the flexible connection.

A wet exhaust system pumps raw water into the exhaust and relies on the tremendous heat absorption that occurs when water is vaporised to produce efficient cooling. Because the wet exhaust discharge is near the waterline, the design must prevent water from entering the exhaust as might occur while man-oeuvring or in heavy weather. An exhaust riser or surge pipe and downwardly-sloped exhaust pipe are effective in keeping water out of the engine. Typical requirements for these features are 1) there must be 12 in (30 cm) of vertical separation between the highest point in the exhaust riser to the LWL and 2) the exhaust pipe must slope downward a minimum of two degrees. The most common problem unique to a wet exhaust system is plugged water injectors. This problem can be identified by checking for hot spots in the exhaust pipe. (See the 'Noise and Vibration Design and Application Guide' for a discussion of muffler performance.)

Engine Fuel Systems

Fuels
The most common fuels used in small craft are diesel and petrol. Bunker fuel oil is used in larger vessels and is made by mixing heavy residual fuel with small amounts of lighter fuels. The resulting fuel is very viscous and contains particulates. Bunker fuel needs to be cleaned and preheated before it can be burned. Diesel (or MDO, marine diesel oil) is a lower viscosity petroleum derivative. Diesel has a lower volatility than petrol; therefore, diesel fuel does not produce potentially dangerous vapours and is more difficult to ignite. This characteristic makes it much safer to store than petrol. This feature, along with the fact that diesel engines do not need an electrical ignition system, makes them very popular for marine applications. Diesels are generally more expensive than petrol engines and do not generate nearly as much power per engine weight compared to gasoline engines. Therefore, racing boats and other high-speed vessels frequently use petrol engines or gas turbines.

There are three categories of diesel engines, high, medium and low-speed. They are defined by their operating shaft speed. High-speed diesels operate above 1,800 rpm, medium-speed diesels operate over a range of 700 to 1,800 and low-speed diesels operate below 700 rpm. Low-speed diesels are used on ships. They are not as efficient as higher speed engines but they can be directly coupled to the propeller and therefore eliminate the need for a reducing gear train. High and medium-speed diesels are used on smaller craft and require reducing gears.

Cetane is the term used to measure diesel fuel's ignition characteristic. Cetane is a measure of the speed at which diesel fuel will ignite. High-speed diesels need higher cetane values whereas medium-speed diesels can burn diesel oil with cetane values as low as 30.

Fuel System
The goal of the fuel delivery system is to safely provide clean and dry fuel to the engine fuel pump. A basic fuel system consists of a tank, filter/water separator and shut-off valves.

The layout of the fuel system plumbing is dependent on the tank location. If the fuel tank is located anywhere from 6 ft (1.8 m) below the engine to 6 ft (1.8 m) above the engine, the fuel supply line is directly routed from the fuel tank to the fuel pump. The fuel return line, in the case of a diesel engine, is plumbed directly back to the top of the fuel tank. If the fuel tank is below the engine, a check valve is included in the supply line to maintain the fuel pump prime. If the tank is above the engine, a check valve is provided on the return line to prevent the tank from filling the engine via the return line.

If the fuel storage tank is located above or below 6 ft (1.8 m), an additional auxiliary tank is normally installed at engine level. This auxiliary tank is plumbed as described above. When the fuel storage tank is located well below the engine, a transfer pump that is actuated by a float switch in the auxiliary tank maintains the auxiliary fuel tank level. The auxiliary tank should have an overflow line in the event that the float switch fails to turn off the transfer pump. In the case of a tank located well above the engine, a transfer pump is not used because the auxiliary tank is maintained full by gravity flow from the storage tank. However, a check valve is added to the engine return line so the engine cannot be filled from the force of the storage tank head. A shutoff valve is also included between the two tanks.

In the case of multiple fuel tanks, the fuel supply line that feeds the engine or engines must be below the lowest tank. The return line must terminate at a point higher than the highest tank. Multiple fuel tanks will sometimes have an equaliser line to maintain an equal level in all tanks.

Engine fuel is one of the leading hazards on a boat – especially when petrol is present. A small leak in a pressurised line will produce a spray that is very dangerous. Not only is it more likely to develop an explosive fuel-to-air ratio, it is extended over a larger area and is more likely to encounter an ignition source. Therefore it is imperative that approved fuel hoses and piping are used. Moreover, they must be protected from anything that could produce a hole, crack or tear. Good design practice calls for:

- Flexible hose should be installed between the engine to any rigid piping. This will prevent engine vibrations from damaging the fuel system.

- The fuel supply line should be as straight as possible. Sharp bends or kinks are not acceptable, as these are likely sources of cracking and leaking. For the same reason, the fuel lines must not be able to chafe against anything.

- Fuel lines must comply with applicable regulations for pressure, heat resistance and permeability.

- The fuel tank vent lines, including any auxiliary fuel tank, must rise above the highest possible fuel level of any tank. This will prevent accidental overflow through the vent lines.

For Diesel Engines

- Check valves on the return fuel line should be mounted vertically to ensure positive sealing.

- The fuel return line should not have any shutoff valves in line. This prevents the line from accidentally being shut off which would cause engine damage.

Engine Air Intake Systems

The engine air intake system must be designed to provide an abundant supply of clean, dry, cool air to the engine. Flow restrictions in the air intake system, along with moisture and heat, will degrade engine performance. Dirt will accelerate the wear of the engine. The suggestions offered here apply to the ventilation of the boat, even for smaller engines where there is no dedicated intake system

Cool air must be routed into the engine

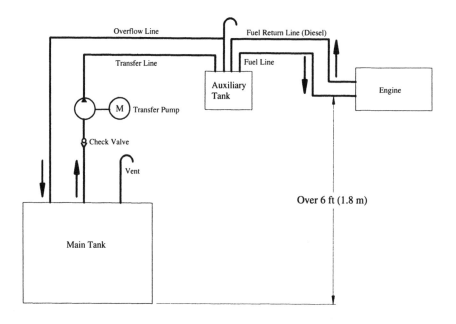

Typical fuel system installation when main fuel tank
lies more than 6 feet (1.8 metres) below the engine fuel
pump inlet. The 6 foot (1.8 metres) number is based on
the typical suction characteristics of an engine fuel pump.

compartment because as combustion air inlet temperatures rise above 100°F (38°C), the engine horsepower decreases by 1 per cent for every 10°F (5.5°C) increase in temperature. Moreover, the heat transferred to the coolant increases by 1.5 per cent for every 10°F (5.5°C) increase in air temperature. Generally, the intake air should not rise more than 30°F (17°C) higher than the ambient air. When an air supply blower is used it should have a capacity of at least 2.5 times the engine air consumption rate.

Air silencers are sometimes used where the boat is operated in a relatively clean environment. These devices simply filter out large particles and reduce the flow sound of the rushing air. Single or multiple stage paper element air filters are used for better air treatment. Often a restriction indicator is installed that warns of high air intake restriction.

Inboard petrol engines must also be equipped with a device that will prevent engine backfires from discharging flames. These spark arresters are attached to the air intake.

The air intake location must be carefully selected so that it 1) does not ingest engine exhaust, 2) does not receive water spray, 3) does not receive accumulated rain or snow. To avoid drawing in engine exhaust the intake must be lower and forward of the exhaust discharge. Engine exhaust drawn into the intake will decrease the amount of oxygen available to the engine and decrease its performance. In the case of diesel engines, ingestion of the abrasive particulates in the exhaust will damage the engine. Large quantities of water, particularly salt water, will also degrade the engine performance. In cold weather, water may freeze on the air filter. The intake should have protective cowls and be above any horizontal surface that collects snow or water from rain or heavy seas. The horizontal surfaces accumulate water and, depending on the action of the boat, can dump the accumulated water down the air intake.

The intake air piping must be designed so that there is little flow restriction. This is accomplished by using the correct size piping for the engine air requirements and the avoidance of 90° elbows, sharp bends and other flow restrictions. The inlet piping must be secure and in the case of turbocharged engines, a flexible line to the turbocharger is required to isolate engine vibrations.

Ventilation

With petrol engines, the most important function of boat ventilation is to remove the fumes. If these fumes collect inside the boat, they can explode if ignited. The other reason to ventilate a boat is to prevent rot and mildew as well as to provide a reasonably comfortable environment for the crew.

Ventilation requires air to be moved from one region to another. This is achieved by a blower or by convective forces that separate hot and cold air by their differing densities. Intake and exhaust cowls and ducts make up the rest of the system.

Bilge and Engine Room Ventilation

Statutes usually dictate bilge ventilation requirements. Good design practice calls for the intake ducts to extend from the intake cowls down to a point around the centreline of the engine. The ducts must be high enough to prevent blockage by bilge water. For engine room/compartment ventilation, the exhaust duct portal should be located towards the ceiling where the hot air accumulates. The cowls must be located so that they are not obstructed during normal operation of the vessel.

Crew Area Ventilation

The availability of hot coffee from the galley may have prevented as many accidents as powerful bilge pumps have salvaged. In the same manner, fresh air ventilation is very important for crew comfort. Crew morale can be improved by such things as good food, dry quarters and fresh air. It is the latter two that ventilation can address. In a wooden boat, however, ventilation has the important role of preventing some wood rot.

The most direct method of providing good ventilation is by inducing a draught with a blower just as is used in bilge ventilation. However, ventilation can be produced by convective flow, where differing density of air (as produced by slightly different temperatures) move relative to one another. This action mixes the air and with outside venting, fresh air can migrate into the boat. A more effective venting system however, will take advantage of the wind or vessel's motion to produced an induced draft as with a blower. Just as with through-hulls, putting holes in the top of boat should cause concern for those operating offshore. Vents must be carefully designed and constructed to prevent the entrance of rain and seawater yet take advantage of relative wind.

Vent design and layout usually concerns itself principally with exhausting air out of the interior (induced draught) rather than drawing it in (forced draught). Air will readily enter from every tiny hole and crack into an area of lower pressure. The role of exhausting vents is to produce this low pressure condition. The exhausting vents must be large and designed in a manner to take advantage of the wind across the vessel produced either by the movement of the vessel or by natural wind.

The most common vent is the dorade vent which is a periscope-shaped tube with a vertical opening above deck. This design uses the air flowing around it to draw air out of the vent. A baffle inside the vent keeps water from travelling below deck. Scuppers in the vent allow water making it to the first baffle to flow out.

These vents need to be located as high above the deck as is practical, to take advantage of the fastest air. Due to the viscous drag of air against the deck and water, a boundary layer is produced. The boundary layer of air is a transitional zone of air whose velocity ranges from zero, where the air is in contact with the deck, to the free, unrestrained velocity well above the deck. Deck machinery and structures also produce vortices that interfere with the proper operation of the vents.

Air intake vents may be simple louvred affairs in cockpit wells, pilot houses or other protected areas. Some boats have a forward facing 'ram' air system for intake air. These must be very well baffled to keep water out.

The advantage of ensuring good exhaust venting is that with the exhaust suction drawing air through the interior, every crack and gap in the boat will add to the intake air venting. Hatches are a part of the ventilation system when weather permits and it usually takes very poor weather before the last hatch is secured.

Compressed Air Systems Design and Application Guide

Reciprocating air compressors are not usually driven by a propulsion engine's power take-off because of the uneven loading that the compressor puts on the engine. Therefore, large compressors usually have dedicated engines and all the previous design guides for engine installation applies to them as well.

Compressed air systems usually have a wet tank, dry tank and an air dryer. The compressed air is routed into a wet tank that allows entrained water and oil to settle. The air travels from the wet tank through an air dryer. Air dryers usually use desiccants, which are hydroscopic chemicals, to directly absorb the moisture. Other dryer designs use refrigeration units and cyclones to condense the water and separate it from the air. After drying, the compressed air is then routed to a dry tank. A check valve separates the dry tank from the wet tank. The dry air passes through a filter and usually an oil lubricator before being used by the pneumatic equipment.

Lack of lubrication is the most common cause of pneumatic machinery failures. The lubricators must not be allowed to empty and must be monitored periodically to ensure that they are dripping or spraying oil into the air stream. Place a hand at the air exhaust of pneumatic equipment and you should feel a slight oil spray while it is operating. Non-lubricated pneumatic equipment does not need a lubricator.

Most pnuematic winches, hoist and engine starters use an air motor with sliding vanes contained within a rotor and cylinder. The most common problem with these air motors is that the vanes stick in the rotor slots or to the surface of the cylinder. This problem is usually caused by lack of air line lubrication, wet or dirty air or lack of use. A heavy spray of oil directly into the motor and a hard hit with a rubber mallet has given new life to many of these motors. This technique should not be used on the newer turbine models. These use an air-driven, high-speed turbine rotor that acts like a centrifugal pump in reverse. These turbine motors are much quieter than sliding vane air motors because the turbine does not contact the containment stator.

Noise and Vibration Design and Application Guide

Noise

Clean air, vast horizons, tranquil seas – yet for many, the rumbling of mechanical noise destroys any fairy tale notion of life at sea. Although engines liberate us from the mercy of the wind or the sweat of our backs, they do it at the cost of adding ugly noise to our environment. Engine noise is the biggest contributor to noise onboard a boat. The biggest problem with noise is its transmission to crew quarters. Unfortunately, the same characteristics that provide hull rigidity, ventilation and good engine performance are the same things that promote noise transmission.

If the note of A above middle C is played on a tuning fork, violin and piano, the fundamental frequency produced will be the same. However, they will have a much different sound. This is due to the other frequencies that are generated along with the fundamental frequency. In the case of a tuning fork, the tone consists almost entirely of a 440 cycles per second (referred to as Hertz, Hz) sound, that is, no other frequencies accompany it. However, in the case of the piano and violin, in addition to the 440 Hz fundamental frequency, these tones also contain sounds with frequencies that are exact multiples of 440. These are called overtones or harmonics and will fall at 880 Hz, 1,320 Hz, 1,760 Hz and so on. Noise is an erratic order of various frequencies. This is objectionable because we do not consider it musical. However, noise can have a stronger physiological impact besides our disdain due to cultural conditioning. Loud, high frequency sounds cause both ear damage and physical stress.

Noise is especially problematic on a boat where the source of the noise is close to the crew. Noise strength varies inversely as the square of the distance. That is, the noise will be nine times as intense at a distance of one foot or one metre from its sources as it would be at a distance of three feet or three metres.

Sound differences are measured in the logarithmic scale of decibels (dB). From the ticking of a wrist-watch to the roar of a shotgun, the differences between the softest and loudest sound we can hear is 120 dB (that is, the softest sound we can hear is about one trillion times quieter than the loudest). Sounds louder than 120dB are felt, not heard by the ear. However, it is not merely the loudness of the noise that is offensive. High frequencies are the most obnoxious and dangerous to humans. The frequency dependence of offensive noise is captured in the standard unit for measuring noise, the weighted decibel scale. Weighted scales take the decibel readings in the frequency range of human hearing and heavily multiply the higher frequencies. The most popular weighted scale is the dBA scale. With this weighted scale, a sound that has a loud 10,000 Hz component would record a much higher dBA reading than does one with a loud 500 Hz component.

Acoustic resonance is the term used to describe the oscillation of an object at its natural frequency. When a tuning fork is struck it will vibrate at a frequency dictated by its rigidity (moment of inertia) and material composition. Resonance is an important concept because the resonant frequency of parts near vibration sources should be designed to fall either at a very low frequency or at one well above the level of human hearing.

The best way to reduce noise is to locate its source and eliminate it at that point. For example, 'engines' do not produce noise, it is certain components or features of the engine that do. Flowing inlet air and exhaust air, cylinder liners, gears and shafts are some of the root causes of engine noise. These sources can be located by acoustic intensity measurements. Acoustic intensity measurements are made with a series of microphones and processing equipment that locate the exact position of a noise source. The approach to noise abatement, excluding air flow noises for the moment, is to first identify the loudest noise source. The offending part may be temporarily replaced with a quieter material to verify that it is the noise generator. Once verified, the object will be redesigned to reduce its noise. Often this involves changing its rigidity to move its natural frequency. This locating process is continued until the noise production is reduced as much as possible. After this is done acoustic panels, mufflers and other more traditional noise abatement techniques can be used.

Noise on a boat is produced, in rough order of intensity by such things as engines, exhaust noise, air inlet noise, pumps and other mechanical equipment, hull noise, the squeaks and rattles of deck hardware, hinges and other miscellaneous items. Fortunately most of the noise is produced in the engine room along with the air intake and exhaust piping where it can be partially isolated.

Basically, external noise abatement is accomplished by using the noise energy to vibrate foam. The soft foam does not transmit the noise well and thereby expends the noise energy and reduces further transmission. Acoustic panels are actually made with a dense material such as lead sheathing attached to the foam. This "tuned" system allows greater noise energy dissipation. Acoustic panels are often configured with a couple of stacked sheathed cores with the innermost sheathing made from a sheet of perforated metal.

Any opening into an engine room enclosed with acoustic panels must be treated to reduce the noise transmission through them. This is most commonly done by lining the openings with acoustic grade polyurethane foam. As the sound waves travel through the opening they get partially absorbed by the foam. Labyrinth designs greatly improve the acoustic foam's effectiveness. A simple version of acoustic panels can be made with marine plywood sheathing and a fibrous glass wool core. Non-marine acoustic tiles and similar material will quickly get damp and may absorb fuel and oil vapours. Acoustic panels mounted on the engine room ceiling and walls will also greatly reduce noise levels.

All piping that penetrates a surface should be sealed with lead sheeting. The best way to treat ducting is to include acoustic foam on the inside of the duct. This prevents the noise from being transmitted to the duct. However, with pipe a different approach is required. Pipes can be wrapped with a fibrous glass wool and a waterproof, protective outer sheathing.

Exhaust noise is the biggest problem and is readily reduced by mufflers. There are two basic types of mufflers, absorptive and reactive. The cheapest and smallest muffler is an absorptive type. These use a wire or fibreglass mesh to absorb sound energy and prevent the sound from reflecting back. These mufflers create a high back-pressure and it is difficult to support the fibre material over a wide area. Reactive mufflers employ acoustic cavities that can be tuned to a single frequency or a range of frequencies. They work by causing a sound wave to reflect off a surface of the cavity that meets the incoming wave in an opposite, and therefore cancelling, phase. For a resonant acoustic cavity, the cavity is simply made with a diameter at least twice the inlet and exhaust diameter. The thickness of the cavity is a quarter of the wavelength of the frequency to be absorbed. Mufflers are usually designed to handle a broader range of frequencies than a simple acoustic filter. Frequently, reactive mufflers are also designed to disperse sound energy by allowing leakage through slots. These are referred to as reactive-dispersive mufflers.

In terms of overall noise reduction, mufflers should be located as close to the engine as possible so that quieter exhaust air flows through most of the exhaust piping. Otherwise, muffler location is unimportant, however, some experiments suggest that locating the muffler halfway between the engine and exhaust outlet is the worst location for overall noise attenuation. The preferred material for mufflers is monel because of its excellent corrosion resistance at high temperatures.

Vibration

Vibration produces sounds just like a speaker. Therefore, reducing vibration will reduce sound generation. Like sound, most vibration is produced by engines and other mechanical equipment. Vibration can be reduced by changing the rigidity as described previously or by vibration isolation. Engines are routinely mounted on elastomeric shock mounts that reduce the transmission of engine vibrations to the engine bed. Elastomers are rated by hardness, quantified by 'durameter'. Engine mounts are usually made with 60 durameter neoprene. Wood also has very good vibration absorption properties.

Torsional vibrations are oscillatory movements that can develop in the engine drive train. The shaft's torsional rigidity, length and the moment of inertia of the driven propeller or gear dictate the frequency that the drive train oscillates back and forth. Torsional vibrations will often manifest themselves by gear rumbling. However, these should not be a problem in a correctly designed drive train. The resonant frequency can be moved above the operating speed of the engine by stiffening the shaft or using a flexible coupling. Whenever shafts are connected by torsionally flexible means such as with gears or splines, they need to be treated separately. Viscous dampers are sometimes mounted to the end of shafts, especially engine drive shafts, to absorb minor torsional vibrations.

Appendix 1
Safety and Technical Standards

I. Safety equipment regulations for small craft are provided in the following documents:

Australia/New Zealand
> Australia/New Zealand Safe Boating Education Group, *Go Boating Safety*.

Canada
> Canadian Coast Guard, *Canadian Coast Guard Boating Handbook*.

United States
> US Coast Guard, *Federal Requirements and Safety Tips for Recreational Boats*.
>
> *Code of Federal Regulations, Title 33, Subchapter O, Subchapter S and Title 46 Subchapter C, Subchapter T*. These are complied in *Rules and Regulations for Recreational Boats* by the American Boat and Yacht Council.
>
> National Fire Protection Association, *NFPA 302, Pleasure and Commercial Motor Craft*.

II. Technical standards and guidelines are provided by the following documents

> *Standards and Recommended Practices for Small Crafts*

American Boat and Yacht Council (ABYC),
3069 Solomon's Island Road,
Edgewater, MD 21037–1416.
United States

The Code of Practice for the Safety of Large Commercial Sailing and Motor Vessels
Marine Safety Agency (MSA)
Spring Place
105 Commercial Road
Southampton SO1 0ZD
United Kingdom

Safety Guidelines for Cargo Ships of Less than Conventional Size
International Association of Classification Societies (IACS)
5 Old Queen Street
London SW1H 9JA
United Kingdom

Other organisations providing technical standards include:

International Council of Marine Industry Associations (ICOMIA)
Meadlake Place
Thorpe Lea Road
Egham
Surrey TW20 8HE
United Kingdom

Yacht Brokers, Designers & Surveyors
Association (YBDSA)
Wheel House
Petersfield Road
Whitehill
Bordon
Hampshire GU35 9BU
United Kingdom

III. The following classification societies provide technical standards.

American Bureau of Shipping
Two World Trade Center
106th Floor
New York N.Y. 10048
U.S.A

Bureau Veritas
Cedex 44-92077
Paris-La-Defense
France

China Classification Society
40 Dong Huang Cheng Gen Nan Jie
Beijing 100006
China

Det Norske Veritas
Veritasveien 1
PO Box 300
N-1322 Hovik
Norway

Germanischer Lloyd
PO Box 11 16 06
20416 Hamburg
Germany

Korean Register of Shipping
Yusung
PO Box 29
Taejon
Korea

Lloyd's Register of Shipping
71 Fenchurch Street
London EC3M 4BS
England

Nippon Kaiji Kyokai
4–7 Kioi-Cho, Chiyoda-Ku
Tokyo 102
Japan

Polski Rejestr Statkow
Postal address: Skr. Pocat. 445
80–958 Gdansk 50
Poland

Registro Italiano Navale
Casella Postale 1195
D+16100 Genova
Italy

Russian Maritime Register of Shipping
191186 St Petersburg
8 Dvortsovaya Nab.
Russian Federation

Hrvatski Registar Brodova
(Croatian Register of Shipping)
Marasoviceva 67
21000 Split
Croatia

Indian Register of Shipping
52 A Adi Shankaracharya Marg
Opp. Powai Lake
Powai
Bombay 400 072
India

Appendix 2
International Standards Organisation (ISO) Applicable Standards

Standard Reference	Description
ISO/TR 4558:1985	Small craft – Rigging screws for stainless steel wire rope – Principal dimensions for forks, connection pins and eye-holes
ISO 4565:1986	Small craft – Anchor chains
ISO 5778:1979	Shipbuilding – Small weathertight steel hatches
ISO/FDIS 5778	Ships and marine technology – Small weathertight steel hatches (Revision of ISO 5778:1979)
ISO 7840:1994	Small craft – Fire resistant fuel hoses
ISO 8099:1985	Small craft – Toilet retention and recirculating systems for the treatment of toilet waste
ISO/DIS 8099	Small craft – Toilet waste retention systems (Revision of ISO 8099:1985 and ISO 4567:1978)
ISO 8469:1994	Small craft – Non-fire-resistant fuel hoses
ISO 8665:1994	Small craft – Marine propulsion engines and systems – Power measurements and declarations
ISO 8846:1990	Small craft – Electrical devices – protection against ignition of surrounding flammable gases
ISO 8847:1987	Small craft – Steering gear – Wire rope and pulley systems
ISO 8848:1990	Small craft – Remote steering systems
ISO 8849:1990	Small craft – Electrically-operated bilge-pumps
ISO 9093-1:1994	Small craft – Seacocks and through-hull fittings – Part 1: Metallic
ISO/DIS 9094-1	Small craft – Fire protection – Part 1: Craft with a hull length of up to and including 15m
ISO 9097:1991	Small craft – Electric fans

ISO 9775:1990	Small craft – Remote steering systems for single outboard motors of 15 kW to 40 kW power	ISO/DIS 12215-1	Small craft hull construction – Scantlings – Part 1: Materials: Thermosetting resins, glass fibre reinforcement, reference laminate
ISO 10087:1995	Small craft – Hull identification – Coding system	ISO/FDIS 12216	Small craft – Windows, portlights, hatches, deadlights and doors – Strength and tightness requirements
ISO 10088:1992	Small craft – Permanently installed fuel systems and fixed fuel tanks		
ISO 10133:1994	Small craft – Electrical systems – Extra-low-voltage d.c. installations	ISO 13297:1995	Small craft – Electrical systems – Alternating current installations
ISO/DIS 10133	Small craft – Electrical systems – Extra-low-voltage d.c. installations (Revision of ISO 10133:1994)	ISO/DIS 13297	Small craft – Electrical systems – Alternating current installations (Revision of ISO 13297:1995)
ISO 10134:1993	Small craft – Electrical devices – lightning protection	ISO/FDIS 13591	Small craft – Portable fuel systems for outboard motors
ISO/FDIS 10239	Small craft – Liquefied petroleum gas (LPG) systems	ISO/FDIS 13592	Small craft – Backfire flame control for petrol engines
ISO 11105:1997	Small craft – Ventilation of petrol engine and/or petrol tank compartments	ISO/DIS 13929	Small craft – Steering gear – Rack and pinion direct link systems
ISO/FDIS 11591	Engine-driven small craft – Field of vision from helm position	ISO/DIS 14509	Small craft – Measurements of sound pressure level of airborne sound emitted by motor craft
ISO/DIS 11592	Small craft – Determination of maximum propulsion power	ISO/DIS 14895	Small craft – Liquid fueled galley stoves

Index